Kay

Forgotten Times Remembered

During The Great Depression

Robert R. Glendon

Bob Glendon

authorHOUSE®

AuthorHouse™
1663 Liberty Drive
Bloomington, IN 47403
www.authorhouse.com
Phone: 1-800-839-8640

First published by AuthorHouse   9/1/2011

ISBN: 978-1-4567-5755-7 (sc)
ISBN: 978-1-4567-5756-4 (e)

Printed in the United States of America

Any people depicted in stock imagery provided by Thinkstock are models,
and such images are being used for illustrative purposes only.
Certain stock imagery © Thinkstock.

This book is printed on acid-free paper.

Because of the dynamic nature of the Internet, any web addresses or links contained in
this book may have changed since publication and may no longer be valid. The views
expressed in this work are solely those of the author and do not necessarily reflect the
views of the publisher, and the publisher hereby disclaims any responsibility for them.

Dedication

To Our Mother Whose Love and Drive
Carried Us Through The Great Depression

TABLE OF CONTENTS

THROUGH MY EYES

Childhood is a passing stage that for good or ill remains with us forever. Even so, adults only grasp the speciality of the wonder years dimly. It is a rare slot in time when the mind congers up events of inventiveness adults have long since disremembered. A child produces images of his/her immediate environment only he or she can touch and love and put away in that secret repository of dreams. Inner space and illusion, peering through a lens that distorts reality and holds back the clock of accountability, is the essence of childhood.

These stories arrive to you through the eyes of a boy I call The Kid. Truth and imagination – struggles during the gloom of the Great Depression and the laughter that drove the blues away. It is about my growing up family and the love we shared.

THE OLD NEIGHBORHOOD
48th Street, Moline, Illinois

Standing ankle deep in the water the short pants kid stared intently at a figure seemingly walking on water far out in the Mississippi river. Eyes squinting against the afternoon sunrays he wondered just exactly how a man could walk on water. When, for crying out loud, would Mr. Erickson take him out? With his toes squishing in the riverbank he remembered Ma giving old Erickson the word. Nothing fancy mind you. "The boy doesn't leave the shore until I say he can." Mr. Erickson gives Ma a scrapy bow and allows as to how the boy is all the time pestering him about the river, but, by golly, he would obey her every command. Ankle-deep was as far as the boy got, but soon his day would come.

A tug pushing several barges piled high with coal chugged up river. The boy marveled how Mr. Erickson just slid along the water as unconcerned as a man could be. The wing dam was a mystery he was yet to know about.

The smell of catfish baking in Erickson's smokehouse caught at the boy's nostrils. Unconsciously, he licked his lips but continued to squint and stare. When the old man got into his boat he waved toward shore and shouted something. Unable to hear him the boy cupped one hand to his ear and shrugged his shoulders. Watching the old man gutting fish didn't do much

3

for his stomach, but the pieces of smoked fish he cadged went down right friendly.

Just then a Rock Island freight whistled a familiar waa, waaa, waaa. The boy ran up the riverbank to the edge of the road in time to catch the engineer waggle his meaty hand at him. He pulled the whistle cord again -- waa, waaa, waaaa. As the freight roared past hot wind twisted the boy's hair and tugged at his pants. By gum, maybe he'd just be an engineer like Mr. Downing. Drive that sucker all the way to Chicago or who knows where.

The wind whooshed as the caboose passed. Watching the train disappear, he made up his mind to ask Mr. Downing about that engineering business. Oft-times when Mr. Downing was hoeing his garden he'd check his pure gold railroad watch every time he heard a train whistle. Real important like, yes siree, Mr. Downing was just the man to see.

The boy skittered back to the shore and sat down brushing off his sandy feet with his socks, lacing up his shoes. Hated his shoes that were last winters high-tops. Ma had cut the tops off and glued on rubber soles she bought down at the five and dime. Darn soles kept coming loose and he flapped along like some idiot. Jeez, he hoped he'd have respectable shoes for school.

He meandered down the shoreline skipping stones on the water. It was a hot buster, but it didn't seem to faze him. There was too much to do in the old East End and summer was running out. Spying a raggedy figure hunched down in front of a shack, he flapped across the road. "Hey, Gene, how's everything?"

Gene pulled his eyes upwards from an anthill and produced a wan smile. He stared at him, questioning like, but said nothing.

"I was down by the river and Mr. Erickson says he's gonna take me out in his fishing boat any day now." Silence. He couldn't figure out Gene. No way. The guy never talked, just stared like he was nutty or something. "Thought you oughta know in case I got drowned in a tidal wave."

Gene grimaced. "Tell ya, Kid, you ain't got a pure chance in hell of sailing with old Erickson."

"Name's Bob not Kid."

Gene flickered a smile. "No different. Why yer Ma'd skin yer hide sure as sin if she caught you on the river."

Seemed like everybody in the East End knew Ma had given Erickson his marching orders. Darn it. At this rate he'd never figure out how the smokehouse man walked on the river. But he knew how to get back at Gene. "School starts in a couple weeks. I'd bet ya a whole nickel yer' pleased about that." The Kid smirked, waiting for a reply, but Gene's eyes went back to the anthill. Sighing, he turned away from the raggedy boy and shuffled off. Probably be a century or two before he ever got a tootie old word from Gene. All in all, Gene was a tough buster to know.

He glanced back toward the shack Gene called home. Poor bugger didn't even have laces for his shoes. Ma said that Gene's Pa had the worst luck of any man she'd ever heard of. Said he was on his "uppers" which meant that he didn't have any soles on his shoes. But, according to Ma, that was table talk and not to be repeated outside the home. *Do You Understand?*" The Kid nodded. What Ma said went.

He looked up and down the tracks then hustled across. One time brother Jack showed him a penny that had been flattened out by a freight train, but The Kid wanted no part of that trick. No Sir, none of that stuff for The Kid. One day he wondered, out loud, why 48th Street didn't go right through to the river road. Johnny pointed out that the tracks were much higher that the street. Simple, said Johnny, any dummy could figure that one out. The Kid decided right then to keep his wondering to himself.

He dropped down to street level and shuffled up to the main drag, 4th avenue. He gathered some rocks from a big empty lot where the elixir man peddled his wellness bottles and where preachers gave out with hell and damnation. Johnny who lived just cattycorner from the empty lot used to sneak across the avenue and spy on the locals. Booze or sermons, all the same they just sit there in a fog and fork out their dollar bills according to Johnny. Brother, The Kid would have given his whole secret stash to live in Johnny's house. He tossed some rocks at not much at all, gave up and watched the traffic.

Bell clanging, a streetcar pulled away from the intersection on 4th avenue. Ma said that new busses were going to replace the trolley cars, but he didn't see any need for that. Trolley cars were the best darned ride a guy could get -- just a chunking along the rails taking in everybody and everything all the way downtown. Once in a while Mr. Wenberg who lived on the corner would give him a piece of chocolate which was a real treat because there wasn't much chocolate in his life. Ma claimed new buses were a sure sign of progress. He had his doubts about that, but he sure wasn't going to argue the point with her.

One time when he was just a shrimp Ma took him with her when she talked to a man in the bank downtown. The banker was all contrite, said something about Ma's stocks being worthless. He didn't understand what the man was talking about, but from the look on Ma's face he knew she had had bad news. Ma held his hand all the way home. Ma was sad.

The boy ran best he could with those darn shoes across the intersection, then sat down on the curb. Watching the Model A's and Chevys chug between the trolley car and the curb, he wondered how come nobody ever got killed. Some of the sodbusters just a choogaed on the horn and revved her up making the ladies jump a mile and yelp. "For land's sake," is what they said, but he bet they wanted to say something more than *that*.

He got up and took a gander at Johnny's house. His pal had been at his grandpap's farm probably stepping in cow pies and cursing a blue streak which Johnny was good at. The Kid smiled. He picked up a rock, and with an exaggerated windup threw it at a telephone pole. Missed, darn it. Tossed again, missed again. Gave up. The boy shuffled along the street, raising dust, thinking about nothing at all. He spotted Officer Larsen's house but didn't see him out in his yard. Officer Larsen worked downtown nights so he had plenty of time to see to it that all was well in the neighborhood. Least wise that was what Ma said. Of course his brothers had a different view. They were a lot older than the boy so where they went and what they did was beyond his years.

He caught sight of the bluff just beyond his house and 5th avenue. Probably Office Larsen spent his time watching out for Blackie Cole, the local bootlegger. What Ma didn't know was that he had his pals spied on Blackie from the branch of a huge elm tree. Fact was he spent his summer days up on the bluff further on in the woods climbing swallow's cliff or wading the creek all the way to the Mississippi, even under the viaduct under Chuck's store, or baking a potato covered with mud in a fire up in the woods or dreaming under the old oak tree doing nothing at all. Or sitting on the back porch listening to and scoring the Cubs slaughter the Boston Braves. Stan Hack was his guy. Best third baseman in the Bigs. Just thinking about playing for the Cubs . . . well it was too darn much to take in for The Kid.

Ma promised to take him to Chicago one day to stay with the Uncle Bill and Aunt Hazel and maybe Uncle Bill would take him to Wrigley field. Gosh, he couldn't wait, but time was running out – school was about to start in a couple of weeks. Besides, money was scarce. Even he knew that. But maybe he could drop a hint the next time the uncles and aunts and cousins came down to see Ma.

The Kid asked why all the uncles and aunts and cousins called her, "Dais," when her name was Helen. Ma smiled and told him that after she was born and lying in her basket one of the Scots cousins said isn't she a daisy and ever after she was known to the Clan as Dais. The Clan? puzzles The Kid. In the Highlands, of course, says Ma. He still doesn't get it so Ma adds,

5 Gower Street, Tain, RossShire, Scotland. The Kid allows as to how he doesn't understand this Clan business. Ma puffs up a bit says, that's my heritage, the Clan Munro, and yours too. Even so we are Americans first last and always. Don't ever forget that. The Kid nods, figures someday Ma will explain it all. For crying out loud, he knows he's an American.

GRENNEL ELEMENTARY SCHOOL

Bud, first row, third seat
Sis, fourth row, in front of teacher

Summer had drifted away on the worn steps of Grennel Elementary School, a gray clapboard one-room affair with a steeple that rested on the dead last street in the East End. Sis and Bud had attended Grennel, but that was way before The Kid's time. Brother Bud had the reputation of a being quick with his fists. "Toughie," as he was called, took on the roughest busters in the East End, but Sis usually stepped in and got him out of scrapes.

Now, like an old man wheezing his last precious breaths, Grennel, a bit mournful and all alone, awaited the chattering little beasts to give it life once again. The Kid liked the cool fall days, and as often happened when walking to school he looked up to St. Mary's Cemetery high on the bluff just past his school. After his Dad died they went to his grave every Sunday, Bud and Jack pulling him up 7th Street hill in a wagon. His father, Ma said, had gone to heaven, and he believed her. But during the winter when the trees were laid bare, The Kid shunned his eyes from the bluff. He didn't like the idea of his father laying in the cold ground all by himself.

Some of the men in the neighborhood like Mr. Downing and Mr. Adams told him what a grand man his father had been. Real smart, too, a respected engineer at Deere & Company. Jack told him that every year Dad pulled the engine on his touring car and rebuilt it in the basement just to make sure the trip east to see Grandpa went according to plan. It made him kinda sad to think that Sis and Bud and Jack knew his father and he didn't.

One time one of the men from Elim Covenant Church, his name was Milt, took him to a father and son picnic where they had races and games and hot dogs and sodas. Ma asked if he had had a good time and he nodded yes. But he fibbed. Milt was a good guy, but he wasn't his real father. He wondered what it would be like to have a father. But Ma and Sis and Bud and Jack made him feel warm and comfortable, and maybe because he was so much younger, important.

He never again went to a father-son picnic.

Wearing a heavy sweater and a floppy cap, The Kid goofed his way to school along with his buddies. He caught sight of the steeple. Its bell that once warned the malingerers to pick up their feet had long been silenced. Bud told The Kid that if anyone rang the steeple bell the whole school would probably fall down. That bothered The Kid, but like most things he didn't like to think about, he forgot all about the steeple. These days Miss Penny stood ramrod straight on the school's tiny back porch clanging an old cowbell. He couldn't hear her yet so there was still time to nuts along with his pals.

Ready for the onslaught, Miss Penny stood as stiff as her white starched blouse. Gray hair done up in a bun and silver-wire glasses gave her an air of authority which was often tested but rarely defied. A brief, soft smile came over her face as she watched Gene Swanson clomp to his seat but it died quickly. If she was any judge of little bodies, and she was, the day promised to be one that would test her self-control. Well, she had better set the tone. Authority, she knew, was easily lost even with the most agreeable ones.

"I want you children to look up to the board."

Eyes shifted to their names in bold black letters. Stars -- gold, silver, and blue -- marked their individual achievements. Smiles, indifference, and hostility marked their faces. Miss Penny read the responses with the certainty of a boa constrictor watching its victims. For now, they were hers.

Miss Penny believed in raw competition. It was, she often told contrite parents, the stuff of which greatness was made. To the wee ones it was a system of embarrassment. Except for Mary Lou Johnson who led the class in gold, silver and blue stars. When another star was placed next to her name she puffed up, self-important like and gave the boys a snaky smile as if to confirm the righteousness of the whole process. On those occasions, Davey Jackson, would let out a sly whistle, not too loud mind you, but just enough to declare the supremacy of the male collection in the classroom. Miss Penny would tap the table with her pointer and murmur something about, "that's enough of that," but secretly she enjoyed the competition.

The Kid liked school, especially the recesses where he led the pack in races, rope climbing and smacking the old ball around. The Kid wondered about Gene though. Why even Mary Lou was faster and quicker than poor old Gene. Those darned shoes of Gene's kept him clodhopping along at a miserable pace. The Kid figured if Gene had a pair of laces he might make a respectable trot, for crying out loud. The guy is pure slow motion that is why nobody wanted to walk with him, let alone race him. Even at recess Gene sort of stayed to himself.

The one guy who don't stay to himself is The Kid's best buddy, Davey Jackson. Davey has a glitter to his eyes that spells trouble. Always into something, he gets away with whatever lie is convenient at the time. Tells his Ma and Pa that he's leading the class with gold stars, and the poor saps believe him. Davey knows they never attend any parent-teacher day, so he is, as they say, home free. Miss Penny keeps her eyes peeled for Davey, but even she isn't sharp enough to hold him in her gun sights all the time.

One recess Davey asks The Kid if he'd like a little excitement. The Kid says what do ya mean and Davey counters with, "If you'd rather play with the girls go right ahead." The Kid had heard this blah, blah, blah, before so he gives Davey an eyebrow and waits to get the bad news. Davey tells The Kid that Mary Lou is just about his speed -- for excitement that is -- so The Kid sucks 'er up and says lead me on or count me in or some such reply. Davey watches Miss Penny like a hawk and when her back is turned he sneaks around to the front of the schoolhouse, The Kid follows, Indian fashion. Davey says he knows how to get up the steeple. Easy as pie, says he. About now The Kid has a wary look on his face, but he's gone too far to back out. So the conspirators sneak into Miss Penny's office and through a door that leads to the steeple. Up goes Davey The Kid follows knowing this could be the end of life, as he knows it.

Once on the steeple platform a whole new world explodes for The Kid. Peaking over the railing, he spies the class at recess, boys on one side of the yard, girls on the other. Tugs are wandering up the Mississippi and freights are whistling past. Davey says, "I told you, Bobby, ain't this fun?" The Kid shakes his head in agreement, but his head weren't the only thing shaking. Suddenly, Davey says, "Watch this," and he pulls out his you-know-what and pees down the open shaft. Davey claims that one-day when he had to take a whiz real bad, that's just what he did. Now he's got the urge every time he goes up. The Kid tells Davey he's crazy as Kenny Murchins, the local idiot, and skedaddles down the ladder, scared as all get out. Davey yells that Miss Penny'll never know, but The Kid figures Davey must be dumber'n a bat because Miss Penny *knows* everything. Besides The Kid spots a wet spot at the bottom of the ladder and knows that if he can see it so can Miss Penny. The busters scamper back down the ladder, circle around to the back yard and join the squealing bodies elbowing each other through the back door. The Kid is quiet for the rest of the day.

After school, The Kid informs Davey that he can pee as much as he wants to but, thank you very much; he'd rather stay in the playground. Davey calls him a scaredy cat, maybe he oughta play with the girls, but The Kid says he's through and that's that.

A week or so later, Davey fails to show up to school one Monday morning, and Tuesday morning, and so on for the rest of the week. The Kid screws up his courage and asks Miss Penny if Davey was sick or something. She says "sort of" which doesn't tell The Kid anything. So on Saturday The Kid trots on down to Davey's house and asks his mother if Davey can come out and play. His Ma allows as to how Davey is confined. That's just what she said, "confined." The Kid lopes on home deep in thought because he doesn't know exactly what confined means. He asks Ma and she says that poor Davey must truly be sick and why didn't she just go on down to the Jacksons to see if she could help in any way. Ma is about the most neighborly person you'd ever want to know. Says that since so many neighbors help her out she's bound to return the favor any time she can. The Kid likes Ma for that.

When Ma returns she's not speaking at all, and when The Kid asks her how Davey is she looks at him all solemn like and mutters he's confined. Which puts The Kid right back where he was before. So he asks Jack and he says that confined means jail time pure and simple. That really disturbs The Kid, thinks he oughta do something about springing his best buddy from the hoosegow, but he never heard of any buster going to jail, no way.

Well siree, when Davey returns to school Miss Penny moves him right up in the front row. Standing smack dab on the top of Davey, she keeps tapping her pointer in the palm of her hand, sort a daring him to make a false move. And when recess comes Davey is, according to Miss Penny, confined to his desk.

Davey Jackson studies up a storm as if he likes his primer, which was nothing but another big lie because he hates book learning with a passion. Brother, there weren't no peeps out of Davey that day, no smirks, no fun at all. Davey Jackson is a changed buster.

After school The Kid catches up with him. "Come on, Davey, what happened? Were you really in jail?"

Davey says, "Shoot fire, wish I had been in jail." What happened was Miss Penny catches him peeing down the steeple shaft. After school was over she gets an arm lock on him, marches him home and informs his Ma and Pa that they got the most wayward malcontent she'd ever had the displeasure to teach. Old Man Jackson lights into Davey right then and there. If Mrs. Jackson and Miss Penny hadn't restrained him, he would have killed his only living son. Then it comes out that Davey wasn't leading the class in gold, silver and blue stars and this so riles up Mrs. Jackson that she fair knocks Davey out of the kitchen. Miss Penny and Davey's old man sit on her until she calms down, but Davey says he never did see his Ma glare at him so.

So happened Miss Penny was trying to be delicate like when she tells them about Davey peeing all over the East End, but when she gets to the part about how he had zeroed in on her she loses her cool and starts banging away on his body. So Mr. and Mrs. Jackson have to hold her down. Poor old Davey says he bounced off so many walls that the kitchen, where the "discussion" took place, must have a hundred dents in it.

The Kid hangs onto every word. This is big stuff, brother. Davey allows as to how he can't sit too well, keeps ducking whenever his old man raises his hand. Says his Ma ain't too bad a slugger either. Says his old man keeps yelling about how he's got the dumbest kid in the East End who on top of it all can't keep his pecker in his pants, and his Ma avoids him like he's got some strange disease. Miss Penny won't give him any recesses, piles books on his desk and orders him to, "READ." Real loud so everybody in the East End can hear. But with all the studying, Davey never gets any stars.

The Kid holds it against Miss Penny, figuring she's a bit too resentful. Besides Davey missed her, didn't he? Truth of the matter, far as The Kid is concerned, is that Davey's a just good old boy who was a might over-enthusiastic.

Finally it dawns on The Kid that he, too, had been up the steeple. Didn't pee, no way, but what adult would believe that! Jeez, he probably would have ruined the family name and been sent to some reform school where the best you might get was a bowl of gruel and a cup of water. Ma would have died of shame. Davey senses the change in The Kid, and says not to worry. Tells him that all the fires in hell won't make him rat on his best friend. The Kid sighs and thinks about what Davey did for him, wonders if he could have been as brave.

The days had sharpened, sweaters turned into coats, outside recess was about to come to an end. Miss Penny kept the little rascals out on the playground as long as she could, but the dreaded days of winter when they were inside all day loomed before her. Miss Penny never touched the devil's brew, but the dreary winter days cooped up with her charges tempted her sorely. She listened to them now crowded around the back porch railing, bunching up, pushing and shoving each other and doing what all to be the first to return to the warm classroom. Then she heard a thump and a yell and was off running. Land's sakes, what now?

Groggy and limp, The Kid lays prone on the back porch deck. He had been sitting on the railing when someone pushed him from behind. He had hit an exposed two by four face first, and his upper lip was swelling. While shooing the children into class, Miss Penny coddles him in her arms. Shoot fire, he don't feel too bad, don't even hurt in fact, so Miss Penny let him stay in school.

On the way home Davey and the busters kid him about his puffed up face, but it don't stop The Kid from taking his sweet old time getting home, just a nutsin' along. It was nearly dark when he marches in the back door. Guy had to waste a good hour or so playing on the way home. Right?

During winter life existed in Ma's kitchen. To preserve precious coal, Ma shut off the hot air registers except for the bathroom and kitchen. Closing the registers was another one of Ma's cost effective measures to squeeze a ton of coal as far as it would go. Each lump of coal shoveled into the gaping maw of the furnace was like a piece of gold to Ma.

When The Kid opens the back door he sucks in an old hound dog sniff hoping for the smell of Ma's All-American vegetable soup, but all he gets is a whiff of dead air. Shucks, he's been daydreaming about Ma's soup and homemade bread toasted to a turn, a class act if there ever was one. Even that old gray-speckled pot simmering on the stove gives out a smile when Ma loads it up with vegetable soup. Shrugging his shoulders and giving out with a disgusted look, The Kid knows he ain't gonna taste his favorite meal.

He strolls into the kitchen ready to give Ma a big smackeroo, but when Ma gets a gander of his face she gives out a shriek and clutches him to her bosom. Which scares the beegeebers out of him. Around the kitchen table The Kid spies Bud and Jack and Sis sitting in a sea of hurt. Mournful pusses look back at him. Sis is soaking her foot in a basin of Epsom salt water, Jack's got his arm all trussed up and Bud has a packet of ice plunked up against his mouth. Seems each of Ma's senior brood had fallen on hard times that day, and as each one arrived home with a foot, arm or mouth to attend to, Ma became progressively depressed. When The Kid bounces in the kitchen with his upper lip about out to the end of his nose, Ma breaks down. "What more," she cries, "can happen this day?" The Kid figures that if she smothers him any harder, she'll be left with one less worry. What with all the tears and rocking he's got that bewildered lost look, that, when Ma inspects his swollen mouth, doesn't help matters one bit.

"Look Ma, it don't even hurt." But the words come out sideways like and Ma decides her youngest is brain damaged for sure. It takes The Kid awhile to convince Ma that he's okay, which helps her cast off the blues.

Finally, Ma recovers her composure and cools down The Kid's lip with some ice chips from the icebox. The Kid wanders around dripping water and slurping his words. Tells Sis that he's okay, but when he spies himself in the mirror, he starts to wonder. The face looking back reminds him of an ape, all distorted, blue and red and puffed up. Now he knows why Ma figures he'd gone goofy, but, gosh darn it, his mind's working on all six cylinders. Poor old Bud, Ma always called him Buddy, sits there all quiet like with two chipped front teeth probably dreaming of the national pole vault record he had missed, or maybe it was Jacky that busted his arm attempting to set the record. The Kid gives Sis a bruised smile, but she starts to sniffle and grabs him for a big hug.

All this time Ma is slamming pots and pans around preparing supper. Tells the tribe they're having creamed tomatoes on toast, which isn't exactly the greatest secret known to man. Ma's winter menu consists of creaming everything she'd canned during the summer and, of course, the ever-faithful oatmeal for breakfast. "It'll stick to your ribs," declares Ma. The Kid's mighty sick of creamed this and that, and, ugh, oatmeal. He swears that if he ever grows up, he'll never eat that glop again, but he ain't about to suggest a change of diet. If Ma says it'll stick to his ribs, then it darned well better. Besides, Sis and Buddy and Jacky are still alive.

It was a rough time for Ma, what with all the brood laying around the place, moaning and sad faced. But the next morning she had them all up, ready to face the day with a piping hot bowl of oatmeal. The Kid's face is kinda distorted, and the oatmeal keeps spilling down his chin like poor old slobbering Kenny Murchins, the imbecile that lived up near The Kid's school. The Kid's slurping kept the conversation down somewhat. Sis and The Boys -- to the neighbors, Bud and Jack were always, "The Boys," -- delivered their attention out the window like there was something important going on outside. Ma declares that The Kid can stay home from school, which is no bad deal come to think of it. But he has her number, figures she's keeping her idiot son under wraps lest the neighbors see him.

The Kid's upper lip backs up to its normal position, but he gets mighty tired of Ma pushing and poking around his mouth to see if his front teeth were all in place. When the snow comes right on schedule he's good as new and ready for winter fun. The weekends were made for fun, sliding down the hills from morning to night.

On Saturdays Ma and her lady friends did their weekly baking, homemade bread, donuts maybe, and once in a while molasses cookies. Ma made scones from a special recipe she had probably smuggled in from Scotland because The Kid never tasted scones at any of his pal's homes.

After a full morning of sliding, The Kid and Davey and Johnny Leach troop into Ma's kitchen like a bunch of puppy dogs waiting to be fed, and Ma shoos them to the basement with orders to hang their wet clothes up to dry. As their coats and scarf's and socks and mittens sizzle on the hot air vents, the rascals run back to the kitchen waiting for the feast. With a grin as big as all get out, Ma asks, "Are you boys hungry?" Which means homemade bread or scones just out of the oven. With fake butter running down their chins, the whizzers argue about who has the fastest sled, daring each other to greater feats of heroism on the afternoon runs. Ma listens to their foolishness and admonishes them to be careful, but her words sail past their heads as so much adult talk. They are the best, no doubt about it.

The Kid brags that his Flexible Flyer may be a hundred years old but is in rare form, sniggers when he reminds Johnny that he had beaten him by a mile that morning. Johnny says yeah, yeah, yeah, bet ya you're scared to take it to the top of McKinley's hill. Davey checks out The Kid, looks for signs of fright. The Kid stops in the middle of a scone gulping and considers Johnny's dare. None of the busters had been up to the top before, but, what the hey, there is always a first time. So The Kid swallows and nods his head okay. Davey lets out a whew, says this is gonna be one terrific ride, that is if The Kid makes it.

With their bellies force fed up to the neck, the whizzers scamper back to the basement and pull their clothes from the furnace vents. Winter clothes weigh a ton. The greater the mass the better, pile it on and wrap it around. Long underwear with a trap door for emergencies, two, maybe three pairs of socks, corduroy pants that squeak and smell up the classroom, wool shirts and homemade knit sweaters, mackinaws that bent the back, long wrap-around scarves, blizzard stocking caps with three holes, two for seeing, one for breathing, rubber boots with metal snaps or high-tops with a pocket knife tucked in the side. No zippers, every piece of clothing buttoned. The axiom of winter clothing is short and simple: Poundage equals warmth.

The Kid looks up McKinley's hill and gulps. Before he left home he slicked up the Flexible Flyers's runners with bees wax and yelled in a loud, fakey voice that his A number one sled is ready to go. But with the steepest slope in the East End packed hard with snow, The Kid wonders if he had been a little too smart. A whole raft of busters are standing around gawking and jeering, waiting for him to meet his doom. Where they had come from is a mystery, but somebody beat the tom-toms. Cripes, the hill is high. Davey gives him a nudge and Johnny says something about history being made. The Kid trudges up the slope, wondering why he gets himself into these things.

Looking down, The Kid maps out his run. When he bottoms out at 5th avenue he has to make a sharp angle turn, first left then right down the alley. Has to miss Jensen's garage that was perched smack dab at the corner of the alley. Taking in a deep breath he runs and belly flops on his Flexible Flyer. The best-darned sled in the East End is about to set a record. Cheers filter up the hill. It's hero time.

Faster and faster he flies down the hill. The cold wind waters his eyes and his vision blurs, but he clutches the steering bar tightly as the sled bounces and hurtles on. He wants to take a swipe at his eyes, but is afraid he might lose control. Holy smokers, he has never gone this fast. What a thrill. At the bottom of the hill he jerks the sled left then gives it a hard right, but it refuses to come around. He pulls the bar as hard as he can but the sled continues to skid sideways. He knows he is in trouble, but he ain't about to give up. Through his blurry eyes The Kid barely makes out the garage. If he can stop the skid he'll make it for sure. "Jump off, jump off," were the last words he remembered.

When The Kid's eyes begin to focus he spots Ma standing by the back door listening to Davey and Johnny stammer and stutter. "Darn near runs right through the Jensen's garage Ma'am. We sure tried to stop him, but his mind was made up Ma'am. It was the bravest thing we ever did see, Ma'am, head first and all."

Ma helps The Kid off the sled and he staggers into the kitchen. But not before hearing a few choice words about little busters taking on McKinley's hill. When she removes The Kid's stocking cap she shakes her head at the bump on his forehead that is now the size of a baseball. The Kid is in fogsville with a dopey smile on his puss. Ma takes a gander at his eyes and is not reassured. The baby browns seem to roll around without purpose, but The Kid ain't worrying one bit. Problem is, when he nods off Ma keeps pulling at his eyelids checking his orbs. Brother.

Ma operates her own emergency ward, pushing slugs of Father Johns' medicine down The Kid's throat before he can argue the point. She holds the absolute belief that a regular dose of Father Johns in the winter wards off colds and assorted dread diseases, so why won't it cure a bump on the head? None of the brood argue with Ma on such matters as home remedies. Got a cold? Well sir, just slap a mustard plaster on the old chest and let 'er work. Or, if the ever-reliable Father Johns fails to do the job, what about a spoonful of castor oil disguised in orange juice? When The Kid eyed Ma squeezing an orange he knew the horrible castor oil was not far behind. It was gaggiest concoction ever known to man or beast.

Ma treats measles, whooping cough, scarlet fever, chicken pox and every infectious disease in the kingdom with all due seriousness. At the first sign of spots the city health department officer would take a peak at the kidos and tack up a sign on the front door.

"KEEP OUT."

In big red letters the neighborhood was warned that the disease of the month lurked inside and would grab anybody foolish enough to enter by the throat. The health department had so many nail holes in Ma's front door it looked as if it had been used for a dart-throwing contest.

Ma believes in disease by the numbers. If one youngster has it then spread it around, by golly. With the bump on his head discoloring by the minute and The Kid half way gone on a trip to funny farms, first Sis, then Buddy and Jacky arrive home looking mighty sickly. The mumps had invaded the East End, and Ma's eldest hadn't been smart enough to duck.

The Kid hears the city health officer pounding a nail in the front door, and as he watches Ma tying kitchen towels around his siblings jowls he figures Ma won't be satisfied until he, too, becomes another statistic chalked up to the mumps. He doesn't think too much of her idea when she pushes him in with the sickies, but when Ma has a determined look there's no naysaying. Ma wasn't satisfied unless the whole crew mumbled along with glassy eyes and heads wrapped up like some Arab tribe sitting in the desert wondering where the oasis went to. Ma's infirmary runs on a group rate plan, cost effective when she has indisposed bodies by the numbers.

But he outfoxes her this time, refuses to attract the mumpy germs. He stays home from school, of course. Can't risk infecting his schoolmates, ha, ha, ha. He had two glorious weeks of nothing to do but listen to Ma's soaps. By the time he staggers back to school under several tons of clothes, his forehead is back to normal.

One morning not long after The Kid said thanks but no thanks to the mumps, Gene clops to his desk and plops his head down, crying softly. He never moves which was not too much different for Gene, but this he time he *never* moves. Mary Lou simply ignores Gene, which she always does anyway, buttering up Miss Penny and answering a ton of questions. But it is hard not to notice that something ain't right.

Miss Penny takes Gene into her office admonishing everyone to study and "reach for the stars." After a century or so Gene returns to his seat and cries all day long. Never even comes out for recess, so The Kid knows Gene is in real trouble.

That night at the supper table The Kid tells Ma about Gene moping around school and Ma tells him that Gene's father had been killed in a train accident. Bud, aka Prunes to the wisenheimers he runs with, allows as to how Mr. Swanson had been drunk and stepped in front of a freight highballing it to Des Moines and was scattered all over town. Jack, who owns the alias Red outside the house, claims that pieces of him are laying all over the tracks.

The Kid stops eating and gets all somber. Ma shushes The Boys, says it isn't their friend who has troubles and besides it isn't right destroying Mr. Swanson's reputation without any facts to back up their fanciful story.

This only encourages the insensitives to greater heights of gore, about how one of their gang found Old Man Swanson's finger all the way downtown, and how all the ladies in the nice homes on river road fainted dead away, and the ambulances were doing double duty rushing them straight away to the loony bin to have their minds checked. The Kid sits there not saying a word, not crying either although he feels like it.

He knows Mr. Swanson ain't any drunk. Not like Blackie Cole who lives up on the bluff. One time Blackie, who is carrying quite a load, booze wise, falls asleep driving up the hill in his Model T flatbed. Blackie and the flatbed go ass over teacup down the bluff, but he ends up on his feet without a scratch and fires up the Model T for another run at the hill. Anyway, The Boys claim Blackie is a bootlegger who swigs his own rotgut twenty-four hours a day, and likely as not Mr. Swanson was sampling some of Blackie's finest. Another lie from his brothers, thinks The Kid.

He used to see Mr. Swanson plenty of times when he was dodging around the river road and Mr. Swanson was a sittin' in front of his shack. Gene's Dad forever asked The Kid how he was, all pleasant like. And The Kid would ask if Gene could come out and play and sometimes he would sit with Gene on the riverbank while Mr. Swanson watched them. After awhile Gene'd amble back into the shack and Mr. Swanson would tell him how much Gene enjoyed his visit, which was fine with The

Kid because he never knew it from Gene, Gene never talking much at all.

The Swanson's had a mangy old dog and even it was sad. He'd mooch over to The Kid for a pet or two, then slump back to the shack and lay down looking over the world with two big old sad eyes. Gene had a couple of sisters, younger than Gene, but they hardly left the shack. Ma mentions the depression but that doesn't mean much to The Kid. He doesn't realize that to Gene and Mr. Swanson too, The Kid lives in a castle and eats three meals a day. But when Ma explains what was what The Kid figures that Mr. Swanson just couldn't take it any longer and stepped in front of the 205 headed out west. One thing for certain, The Kid refuses to believe Gene's Dad was a drunk.

The next week Gene Swanson comes to school but he just lays his head on his desk about all day long. The Kid guesses he ought to say something to him, and when Gene goes outside for recess The Kid screws up his courage. He finds Gene sitting by himself staring into space. The Kid sidles up and says how sorry he was to hear about his Dad's accident.

"Bobby, he ain't any drunk like people are saying."

The Kid says that he knows that's the truth for sure, and that he feels real bad and hopes Gene and his Mom will be okay which, under the circumstances, is a long speech for The Kid. Gene just puts his head down between his legs and don't say no more so he wanders off feeling sad.

Well, somewhere near the end of the week, during one of the recesses, The Kid spots Miss Penny and Gene in the front of the school talking to a man who Ma once said ran the schools. Gene walks away holding the man's hand, head down shuffling like always. The Kid sees Miss Penny take out her handkerchief and dab, delicate like, at her eyes. The Kid knows something important has happened and he feels empty not knowing what the grownups have done to Gene. After classes have been dismissed for the day, he sits in his seat not knowing exactly what to say. Miss Penny approaches his desk, a worried look on her face. She sits down in one of the seats next to him and smiles. "Well, Bobby, what seems to be the problem?"

The Kid stammers something about seeing Gene leave the school with a man and not coming back. Wasn't talking too well at the time. Miss Penny gets all motherly and puts her hand, tender like on The Kid's hand. "Well, Gene and his mother and sisters are going back home to Iowa. They'll be living with Mrs. Swanson's folks on a farm. I think that's a grand idea, don't you?"

The Kid mumbles about how that sounds fine and he just wanted to know if his asking was okay with Miss Penny. She says that his caring about what happened to Gene was mighty fine with her so The Kid feels better and walks to the front door. He turns in time to see Miss Penny pull out her handkerchief and turn her back.

The guys are waiting for him as they're sure he's in some kind of trouble, staying after school and all that. They can't wait to find out what kind of punishment he got, musta been a big one, for sure. But The Kid tells them about Gene Swanson leaving town for Iowa and Miss Penny saying Gene's just gonna be just fine. Davey lets out a hoot and mouths off about Mr. Swanson being a drunk and a lazy galoot who slugged down too much of Blackie Cole's booze and got hisself killed. The Kid takes off after Davey yelling something fierce. Says he'll beat the stuffings outa Davey for telling such lies. Davey screams back that he's sorry and that he'll never ever say anything bad about Gene's dad again.

Panting, The Kid stops and yells, "Promise."

Davey stops and promises on the grave of his dead dog, which is a solemn promise if The Kid ever heard one. So they walk home friends again, closest pals, exchanging their secrets like before. But The Kid knows the story about Gene's dad being a souse will never die, he just knows.

The Kid's mighty quiet when he gets home, and Ma notices right away that something is amiss. He explains that

Gene Swanson was going to some farm in Iowa, and that Mr. Swanson ain't any old drunk and all that. Ma wants to correct her youngster's language, but decides the time isn't right. The Kid wasn't crying or anything, but he couldn't see so good because he felt awful.

All of a sudden Ma's voice gets all soft like, and she tells her youngest not to worry, that he should remember that when he is feeling sorry for himself there is always somebody else who is hurting more than he is, and that life has its share of hurts which you have to stand up to. The Kid figures nobody knows more about hurts than Ma and when he looks back at her through the kitchen door she has her handkerchief out dabbing at her eyes, just like Miss Penny.

The Kid lays in his bed in the attic, like always listening to the waa, waaa, waaaa of the train whistles and dreaming about where the trains were headed and what the people were doing in those far away towns. But that night, and for a long time afterwards, when the train whistles blew their mournful cry, The Kid couldn't help but think about Gene Swanson and the rotten trick life had played on him. When all was silent, The Kid would shut his eyes tightly and conjure up the image of the raggedy boy who clumped along, but in time Gene Swanson's face drifted away. Oh, once in awhile when he tied his shoelaces, when the train whistles were lost in his childhood dreams, he remembered Gene and would pause, just for a moment.

MA

The brood is sitting around the kitchen table having a meal of one of Ma's favorites, creamed tomatoes on toast or some such concoction. Ma is in a good mood and she begins to tell about their train trip to Chicago to see the rest of the Munro clan when Sis and Buddy and Jacky were just shrimps.

"Before," she turns to The Kid, "you ever saw the light of day." This interests The Kid. He likes Ma's stories.

It seems Ma has the chicks all slicked up and ready to board the ten o'clock special leaving the depot for Chicago. According to Ma railroad men really prided themselves keeping the trains on time. The image of Mr. Downing pulling out his railroad watch checking whether old number 99 was on time skips through his mind.

The special, Ma says proudly, pulls in exactly on time and she gets the troop on board and seated properly. She had purchased her ticket at the depot, and, hoped, once more to pass the kiddos off for a free ride. The rule, Ma says, is that children under the age of five ride free. Sis is six, but Ma figures she is small for her age and if she tosses the conductor a smile and a nod, he won't ask any silly questions about how old the children are. The Kid is hanging on her every word.

So down the aisle marches the conductor smiling and punching tickets and wishing everybody a nice trip. He spots Ma and tells her what a fine bunch of youngsters she has and sticks in his punch line, "Just how old are the little treasures, Madam?"

Before Ma can get a word out, Sis pipes up all perky-like and blabs, "Why I'm six and Buddy is five years old today."

The conductor pats Sis on the head and says, "Why, what a smart girl. You must be a comfort to your mother."

Ma is fit to be tied as she not only has to pay for Sis but Buddy, too. This event happens before the depression and Ma isn't exactly struggling for cold hard cash, but to her it's the principle of the thing. She's in a corner and has to cough up two half-fares. When the conductor leaves, Ma gives Sis the old what for -- like, "Speak ONLY when you are spoken to," and, "Mind your Ps and Qs."

A bit forlorn, but a darned sight wiser, Sis wonders if she will ever see the ripe old age of seven. Watching Ma peeling off an entire fortune isn't the most heartwarming sight in the world.

But now Ma is telling the story on herself and laughing until the tears run down her face and the brood is enjoying themselves no end. Even though he is filled to the eyelids with Ma's creamed this or that on toast, The Kid thinks it's pretty keen when Ma tells stories on herself.

But Ma's good humor wasn't about to last too long. There was always some con artist coming to the door selling the latest nonsense, "that the lady of the house just couldn't do without," but Ma could spot a con quicker than most anybody on earth. She talked about the highbinders that tried to get a foot in the door and how she fended them off and how the brood had to be on constant alert for these no-accounts because guarding the family purse was one of the highest duties known to man.

Sis takes this all to heart, but Buddy and Jacky –- to Ma they were Buddy and Jacky -- stifle grins knowing that she had about a dozen padlocks on her pocketbook and only she had the combinations. Even so, she didn't always win these battles. The Household Furnace scam got her for sure.

Ma's furnace, a huge octopus-like monster with great round ducts, wandered up to the first floor rooms. Until Bud and Jack were old enough she shoveled coal during the long, cold winters, banking the fire at night with expertise, removing clinkers the size of Pete Benson's Model A with long tongs, coughing all the while from the noxious fumes. Problem was the furnace was so old it was about ready for the Smithsonian. With Ma complaining about all the trouble she had with it last winter, The Kid figures the ugly monster was about to be consigned any day now to the furnace graveyard, or where ever old furnaces go.

It so happens that disaster struck on one of those hot busters when Ma is in the kitchen sweating over her yearly chore canning her crop from the vegetable garden. Each summer she measured success by the number of Mason jars she filled with tomatoes, beans, turnips, etc. First she washed the jars in steaming hot water to make certain they were sterile then added super hot water to the vegetables packed in the jars. It was a down year if she did not have over a hundred jars of tomatoes. Slaving away in a hundred plus degree kitchen fed us during the winter.

When the furnace scam-artist shows up at the house offering Ma a, "free check, Ma was ripe for the sales pitch. Her first mistake was letting the shyster in the door, but he sold her a load of bushwah about how the furnace probably only needed a first class cleaning and how trusted his company was in the community and how much he admired the little shaver peeking over the back porch rail.

The Kid dislikes the fast talker immediately, distrusts slickers that all the time fawn over Ma's kiddos. The scudder and his partner who had been hiding behind the back yard elm tree hit the basement as if they had found a gold strike. After a couple days inspecting and tearing it apart the furnace lay in pieces, a giant jigsaw puzzle waiting for someone to put 'er back together. When they call Ma downstairs she about has a heart attack. Not to worry grins the highbinder, "What you need, Madam, is a brand new furnace because this one is completely shot. Repairs are impossible."

Ma's mouth dropped about a foot, and for a second or two she can't get the words out. Well Siree, Ma might be taken in by a fork-tongue once, but not twice. She chases those deadbeats out of the basement, swatting their backsides with a broom and yelling a few choice uncomplimentary accusations about how they preyed on poor widows with four mouths to feed and where in all get out did they think she could buy a new furnace let alone repairs. The cheats were last seen hightailing it down the alley arguing with one another about how you couldn't make an honest buck these days without being branded public enemy #1.

Ma doesn't let it sit there either. She gets on the tom-toms

30

and passes out the wanted notices. Before the day was done the entire East End is laying for the crooks that tried to scam Ma. They tell Ma how much they appreciate her quick response, but Ma is mighty subdued when she goes to bed that night. What in the world is she do?

The next Saturday a few neighborhood men, husbands of Ma's closest lady friends, come in to take a look at the mess in the basement. They tell Ma that they can get a hold of a used furnace and, if it's okay with her, they will install it before winter. Ma is both elated and downcast, she knows she has to have the furnace, but even a used one would break the annual budget.

"How much is it?" Ma asks quietly. Mr. Wenberg pulls at his cap and tells the straight of it. "Won't cost you a red cent, Mrs. We got the furnace for free."

Tears arrive in Ma's eyes. She knows darned well the men had to pay something for the used furnace and that more than one neighbor won't eat so grand this week, but she accepts with grace, promising herself that some day she will return the favor. At the next social get together she'll tell her lady friends how much their friendship means to her. Helping out, Ma declares, is the most neighborly thing a person can do.

About this time Sis graduated from high school and had an interview with the plant manager of the Harvester Works for a secretary's job. Not about to let this opportunity to slip by Ma escorts Sis to the interview. What she said to the plant manager has not been recorded for history, but Sis, praise be, was hired. Some months later Sis was offered a better paying position at Deere & Co. headquarters. Back to the plant manager goes Ma with Sis in tow. Ma told him directly as can be that although Sis had an opportunity for more money at Deere & Company headquarters she would stay in her present job as he had been kind enough to hire her in the first place. He told Ma that there were two hundred girls waiting for Helen's job, and she was free to accept the position at headquarters with his blessings.

To Ma, loyalty was an absolute virtue, as deeply ingrained in her Scottish character as her love for her children.

So, with the family coffers on the upswing a few household improvements were in Ma's plan for a brighter future. She orders a roll of linoleum for the kitchen floor. It was tan with little ant-like specks running around in a crazy pattern. Ma likes it a lot. The Boys clear the table and chairs out of the kitchen and remove the hot air register that rested on the floor by the doorway opening into the dining room. Bud, who was blessed with smarts, measures the floor and cuts the linoleum to fit exactly. This is a ticklish job and The Kid admires his eldest brother because one mistake and he'd be sleeping in the garage for a year or two.

Ma had this character quirk that demanded everything be done as perfect as can be. She had no use for sluggards or malcontents, and, by example, pounded it into her brood that work was not simply a necessity but a virtue of uncommon worth.

Anyway, the linoleum is stiffish and hard to bend, so after The Boys roll it over the floor Ma says it has to set until it snugged down just so. Problem was that it covered the open register hole, the exact spot where everybody stepped when going into the dining room.

Ma judged the danger all right, announcing to the whole kit and caboodle to "watch their step." Morning noon and night she gave out with her laser stare and waved her finger at them menacingly, "When you walk in here for heaven's sake don't step on the hot air register hole as the grate has been removed and if you break the linoleum you will ruin the whole floor and if that happens I'll skin you alive." Ma watched the four heads bob up and down, swearing everlasting vigilance. When Ma made a pronouncement, they listened. Time and time again, it proved to be the best way to stay alive.

While all this activity is going on The Kid plops his rear on the back porch swing too beat to even get the latest skinny from Russ down at the gas station. It's a real hot buster; the kind Old Erickson calls dog days. The Kid is penciling in his favorite Cub players, Billy Jurges, Billy Herman, Augie Galan, and Stan Hack on a yellow pad. It's important that he record their hits and runs. When the game is on The Kid resides in another world.

Ivy had just been planted on the outfield walls of Wrigley field and he wishes, nay prays, that one day before he entered that great diamond in the sky one of the Scots clan from Chicago would take him to a game. At the moment the Cubs were thrashing the Giants 4 to zip and Charlie Root had his great curve working. The Kid couldn't look more like an angel had a halo ringed his head.

Suddenly, a loud thud and horrible scream pierces his ears. The Kid leaps from the swing and runs into the kitchen. Ma sits askew the register opening, one leg dangling in the basement, the other leg resting on the floor at a terrible angle. In her usual rush through the kitchen she had forgotten the forbidden area, and now sits there in a daze all scrunched up. She busted out the hot air duct from its connections, and her right leg, covered with soot, hung uselessly between the floor joists. She was stuck as stuck could be. The Kid could hear the duct clanging as it bounced out of control hitting the basement rafters.

Ma is in awful shape, all crunched up, unable to free herself. The Boys come hightailing to the rescue. Bud takes the basement steps five at a time and pushes Ma's leg up while Jack and Swede grab her by the arms and pull up for all they're worth. She is hurting something fierce, but the first thing she does is check the linoleum. The brand new linoleum is busted sure as shootin', but it showed cracks only up to the edges of the register opening. Bud cuts the linoleum like the master craftsman he is and drops the grate onto the hole. Perfecto.

Praise the Lord, Ma cries.

It is awful quiet around the supper table. The brood sit silently eating one of Ma's specials, glancing at one another but mainly staring out the kitchen window. The Kid considers complimenting Ma about how wonderful the new linoleum looks, but the words are stuck fast in his throat. Bud and Jack have their heads bowed and Sis sits ramrod straight in her chair. Brother, it was a miserable meal.

When she finishes her plate, Ma pushes her chair back, smiles, and says, "If I told you once, I told you a thousand times -- DON'T STEP ON THE REGISTER." Then she laughs and laughs. The brood gathered around her and asked how she is feeling and slip her a kiss and laugh as if happy days are really here again.

She limps around for a week, but like the pros say, you play with the small hurts. Like always, Sis, Buddy, Jacky and The Kid give Ma a kiss when they depart for the great outdoors. Even when all the Munro Clan visited from Chicago the kissing business never seemed to end. So this evening as Ma limps around clearing the dishes The Kid gives her an extra big hug and a kiss. She likes that.

Ma had a bunch of special lady friends she called by their last names -- Hancock, Vergane, Haley, Levins, to name a few. They gathered together once a month to play cards and fill each other in on the current state of affairs. Russ down at the gas station said their meetings were pure gossip, but The Kid figured if anyone knew anything about gossip it was Russ.

Anyway, each of the ladies brought a "dish" which cornered the market on all the goodies that could be found in the East End. Between bites of jello salad and tuna delight the state of the neighborhood and all the miscreants therein received their undivided attention.

It was at these socials that Ma voices her concern over the lousy state of affairs in the country. While they fork up generous portions of home-baked goods, the good ladies encourage Ma's political interests. She believes devoutly that President Roosevelt is the savior -- with a capital S -- of the country. So she makes up her mind she'd help get every Democrat in the state, county and town elected. It was the least she could do for the grandest man that ever lived.

That year Alf Landon, a true blue son of Kansas, campaigned against President Roosevelt. One day The Kid spots Landon's train highballing 'er through the East End. Along with the other busters waiting to catch a glimpse of the famous man from the west, all The Kid sees is a hand waving from a window and a flurry of campaign buttons tossed from the train. The Kid grabs one. With his face smiling out of a sunflower, Alf Landon looks pleasant enough. It's as close to the candidate as The Kid ever gets, and for a little buster the button was big stuff indeed.

The Kid races home and tells Ma all about his near sighting of the Republican all the way from Kansas and shows her his prize possession -- the Landon campaign button. The Kid has seen Ma upset a time or two, but her reaction puts him up against the wall.

"Bringing that *thing* into this house." Disgusted is hardly the word.

The Kid looks around and sees a whole warehouse full of Roosevelt buttons so he allows as to how one measly Landon button won't desecrate the homestead. Ma sets him straight, says when he is earning the cold hard cash and running the house then he can bring in any darned button he wants, but until that time she has the say of the matter and, "DO YOU UNDERSTAND?"

The Kid isn't any Einstein but he's got more than a few cogs in his gears so it was pretty clear to him that Ma wasn't about to put up with Mr. Landon's puss smiling out of the sunflower. He takes his prize and hides it in the garage, figures that if Landon wins the election Bud might want to wear it when one of his big ideas is recognized and he's invited to the White House. He tries not to think what Ma might say about that.

As Ma is busting around the kitchen preparing dinner, The Kid assesses her mood. Ma's a mover in more ways than one. When she believes in something or somebody she isn't about to stand around letting moss grow on the north side of her convictions. Her attitude has been on the cool side ever since he showed up wearing the enemy campaign button, and he prays for an idea that would restore his favorite son status.

The Kid informs Ma that the school principal had decreed that a mock presidential election would be held in the school auditorium and what did she think about them apples? Being her most serious self, Ma passes her eyes across the table paralyzing The Kid from the neck up. "You *are* speaking for the president are you not?"

Why, The Kid mutters silently, "Can't I keep my big mouth shut?" Aloud he says, "Hadn't given it much thought, Ma."

"Well, do so," Ma demands.

The Kid gets the big picture, knows his life will be on hold unless he gets in line with Ma's political program. The Kid shakes at the thought of speechifying before all his classmates, but if it means making Ma happy he'll get off the dime and do 'er. So he stumbles through a speech and President Roosevelt wins the school election by a zillion votes. Ma's pleased as punch, figures her youngest is a political comer for sure.

At the next big Democratic rally, Ma drags The Kid down to the Swedish Olive Hall, tells him to pay attention to the party power brokers. The Kid's been there before. Listening to all the longwinded local pols imploring the precinct committee captains to get out the vote was about as much fun as listening to Ma claim that all the starving children in some alien country would be happy as a lark eating the asparagus he was gagging up on his Sunday plate. For crying out loud she even hid the noxious glop under his potatoes.

Anyway, the only thing that saves The Kid's sanity is the huge table in the rear of the hall loaded down with sandwiches and the coolers filled with soda pops. While Ma soaks up all the helpful hints about getting out the votes, he sidles around to the sandwich table, eyeing the ham, cheese, baloney and peanut butter. It takes a while to make the big decision, but finally he settles on a big baloney and cheese. Then he addresses his attention to the tubs of soda bottles. All his favorites are icing down nicely, but when he spots a cream soda his choice is made.

The Kid stations himself right close to the table ready to pounce once the blathering mercifully ends. Unconsciously, his tongue whets his lips in anticipation. His stomach aches for the baloney and cheese being washed down with an ice cold cream soda.

Just before the political fathers run out of gas, Ma says she wants to introduce The Kid who, she says proudly, just won the school election for President Roosevelt. Everybody claps and wants to meet the wonder boy. Trapped. He scrunches up against the back wall, but Ma drags him up front where he produces a shaky smile and palms more than a few sweaty hands.

While all this is going on, the free loaders beat a retreat to the food leaving The Kid at the speaker's platform. He watches in horror as the sandwiches and soda pops vanish. By the time he gets to the table the only sandwich left is peanut butter, and worse yet all the cream sodas are in the paws of the city fathers. Disgusted, he stares at the peanut butter sandwich, thinks for a second that he just might take it home to brother Bud who swallows the gooey stuff by the tons. Politics, he decides, is full of baloney, and not the sandwich kind either.

When the day to cast ballots arrives Ma is up at the crack of dawn chasing down voters too old or lazy to do their solemn duty. The voting booths stand inside McKinley school's gymnasium. The Kid watches Ma carting in half the infirmary who hadn't seen the light of day for a century or so. Ma helps the golden oldies down the steps and explains where they should put their "X" -- Democrat, of course -- just in case their feeble scrawls slip into the enemy's column. To make sure the Xs are scored for the Democrats, Ma gets permission to help the blind, the dimwitted and the don't-give-a-hoots.

Her adversary is Pete Benson, the local Republican precinct committeeman. Besides Ma being the neighborhood Democratic pusher, Pete let it be known that Ma should have better control over The Boys and the Neanderthals they run with. According to Pete, a rock solid Republican administration would make life a whole lot safer on the streets.

Like Ma, Pete's out on the hustings getting out the vote. The Kid spies his Model A chugging up the school hill with its springs hitting rock bottom and Mrs. Sperling sitting queen-like in the back seat. How Pete packed old lady Sperling into his Model A astonished The Kid. Mrs. Sperling was a biggie, real whale sized in fact. With sweat seeping through his shirt, Pete pulls and tugs and finally pries Mrs. Sperling's bulk out the car door. The Model A springs bounce back to where they oughta be and Davey and The Kid fall all over themselves laughing as Pete assists another sure vote to the polls. The sight was something to see.

Next time The Kid spots Ma rushing up to the polls he asks her how things are going. Ma says the election might just be close because Pete Benson is bringing in people who last voted in the Civil War, or maybe the Revolutionary War for all she knows. The Kid knows everybody in the East End, and some of the old geezers in Pete's custody were just this side of boot hill. Course, some of the basket cases Ma hauled to the polls were last seen shaking hands with Abe Lincoln, so all in all, as Davey said, it was dead heat. Yuck, yuck, yuck!

The Kid decides the situation is more serious than one of Davey's stupid jokes, and he's feeling sorry for Ma and her cohorts who were carrying on as if life and death depended on bringing in the Xs for the Democrats.

On the way home from school The Kid spots Pete's Model A parked in front of Mr. Burley's house. Old Man Burley's hadn't seen the sun's rays since World War I, but he knows for certain Pete is in there giving the old geezer a shot of something zitzy just to get him to the polls alive. He figures if Ma is having all that trouble boosting the president over the 50 percent marker, maybe he oughta help the cause along.

It's still a couple hours before the polls close, and he wonders what would happen if Pete was unable to deliver his quota of oldies on time. Smiling to himself, The Kid ducks down on the far side of the Model A and lets out the air in the rear tire. He slinks away Indian fashion, no one the wiser.

Late that evening when the local votes have been counted Ma arrives home happy as a bee stinging up nectar from the flower of success. The Kid learns that the Donkeys walloped the Elephants by a zillion votes. Snoozing in bed listening to the mournful cries of the freight trains, The Kid drops off with a smile on his puss.

At the breakfast table Ma has the radio blaring. Seems President Roosevelt is a winner in a landslide. Ma declares it is a great day for America. The Kid looks at Red and Red gives him a wink. With Ma talking about and listening to the latest returns at the same time, The Kid and Red undo her apron strings, and then slicker'n butter they tie the strings to the back rungs of her chair. Red asks Ma if she has any more of that stick-to-your-ribs stuff, and when Ma gets up so does her chair. "You divels," she cries. The whole brood give out with a big whoop-de-do, and Ma tosses off a fakey madder-than-hops look. The Kid is enjoying the scene no end as tying Ma's apron strings to the back of her chair is his all-time favorite trick.

When Sis and his brothers depart they give Ma a hug and a grand smacker. The Kid watches all this good time feeling with a great deal of satisfaction, and when it's his time to skip off to school he can't contain himself, tells Ma that he, too, helped out President Roosevelt. Ma thinks The Kid is talking about his speech at school, interrupts The Kid saying how much the city fathers appreciated what he had done for the country, but The Kid explains that he *really* helped out, tells her about throwing a monkey wrench into Pete Benson's Model A and how do like that Ma?

Happy days blew out of the kitchen as fast as the air swooshing out of Pete's rear tire. Ma's face resembles a ripe tomato. She warns him to keep his mouth shut and to come home straight after school with no fooling around on the way and if he didn't, she would give him away to the ragman. The Kid gulps, gets the idea that maybe he hadn't been so gosh darned smart after all. It was a long day in school. Nothing funny happened at all.

Contrite as all get out The Kid shuffles home slowly into the kitchen of doom. Ma's waiting for him, says that what he had done was wrong, either you play fair or life isn't worth a hoot.

"Now young man, you march yourself directly up to Mr. Benson and apologize. And," Ma waves a finger at him, "stop by Miss Epperson on the way back." Wow, Miss Epperson, too!

The walk to the Benson house was only a few blocks, but it was the longest, slowest trek The Kid had ever made. Standing with his hand on the front gate he hesitates, recalls Bud's words of wisdom: "If you've done something wrong, take your punishment like a man. Don't be hangdog about it. And stand up straight for crying out loud."

A shiver runs through his body then he pulls his eyes off the ground, a pathetic little figure trying to screw up his courage.

"Something you wanted to say, Bobby?"

Pete Benson, his face hard as stone, stands on the front porch. The Kid stammers and shuffles his feet. Pete beckons him to the porch and they sit down on the swing. Words stick in The Kid's throat.

"I let the air out of your tire yesterday, Mr. Benson." Silence.

"I'm sorry I caused you so much trouble." Sit up straight, darn it, sit up straight.

"Why did you do that, Bobby?" Stern face, hard words.

"I . . . I thought I was helping Ma." It wasn't getting any better. The Kid begins to sweat.

"And what makes you think your mother needs that kind of help?"

Jeez, what was he supposed to say? Keep your head up -- stop staring at the floor. "It weren't Ma's fault, Mr. Benson. It was just . . . me. Honest."

"I know it wasn't your mother's doing. But how do you think she feels now?" Pete Benson felt The Kid stiffen then his voice softened. He put his arm around him.

"Well, I hope you have learned a lesson young man. I've been thinking about what I ought to do about your prank, but it seems to me that flat tire taught you something." Pause. "The way I see it, this is the quit of it."

Surprise mixed with hope lit up The Kid's face. Maybe he wouldn't have to do Pete Benson's chores for the next forty years after all.

"One more thing. Another Mrs. Sperling in my Model A would have busted its springs and blown out all its tires." Pete Benson chuckles, "All in all, Bobby, you probably did me a favor."

A tentative smile crosses The Kid's face, but then Pete becomes serious again. "I want you to remember one thing. When you elect a president he is the president of all the people, and when a Republican wins the next election and sits in the White House he, too, will be the president of everybody." Pete Benson's eyes bore in on The Kid's. "Do you understand?"

"Yes, sir." The Kid looks at Pete Benson with respect, figures he is a right fair man.

"Now, be off with you." The Kid stands up and offers his hand just as he was supposed to do. Pete smiles, "And say hello to your mother for me." The Kid scampers off relieved. At the corner he turns back to the Benson house and sees Mr. Benson still standing there, smiling. The Kid waves and Pete Benson waves back.

On the way back home -- going a smidgen faster than on his outward journey -- it dawns on The Kid that Pete Benson *knew* he was coming. And since only Ma knew he had let the air out of Pete's tire then it figured Ma had told Pete about it. Probably told Pete about what a worthless son he was, and Mr. Benson had agreed with her. Shoot fire, Pete didn't have to punish him. He knew Ma would see to that. So now The Kid started worrying about what Ma would do to him.

Then he remembered Miss Epperson.

Mamie Epperson was one of Ma's good friends. She was an ancient crone. Her thin emaciated body, sharp nose and bird quick eyes gave her a witch-like appearance. She had retired from teaching and lived in a dank, dark house The Kid avoided whenever possible. The curtains were always drawn as if shadowy secrets to gruesome to bear the light of day lurked inside.

Ma considered Mamie Epperson the smartest person in the neighborhood. They were forever talking politics and exchanging views of the world. When Ma had a problem that was kinda deep -- you know, about life and values and that sort of thing -- she trotted over to Mamie Epperson's to get the right of things. Which was okay for Ma, but Jeez, not for The Kid.

He knocked lightly and the front door opened.

"Bobby. How nice. Do come in."

Standing politely at attention, The Kid peeked around the gloom expecting Dracula to pop out from behind the drapes. He stared at Miss Epperson's shoes wondering why Ma had sent him to see her. Then it came to him -- *he* was Ma's biggest problem.

"I have a book here for you."

The Kid took the book gingerly, apprehension kneading his brow. *SUNBEAMS*. It was huge.

"Land's sakes, there's nothing to be afraid of. Here, look at me." The Kid glanced up slowly catching the eyes of Mamie Epperson zeroing in on him. His skin had that creepy, crawly sensation that spelled doom. Dracula was behind the drapes he just knew it.

"I have the poems marked for you to memorize."

POEMS! MEMORIZE! It would take him a century to memorize all those poems. The Kid groaned.

"What did you say?"

"Nothing Miss Epperson."

"Your mother, bless her soul, agrees with me that you have a lot to learn about life. Especially what it means to be fair. LOOK AT ME! That's better. I'll expect you here after school until I am satisfied you know right from wrong. How long that takes depends on you."

"Yes, Miss Epperson." Eyeing the drapes, The Kid backs out of Mamie Epperson's dungeon of a house. Then, setting an East End sprint record, he runs home.

Ma sits him down and talks to him straight out, but no yelling, no threats. The Kid has been force fed with the idea that the only real thing you carry with you all your life is your good name, and now, he decides, his is gone forever. Otherwise why did Ma bring Pete Benson and Mamie Epperson into it?

Ma goes directly to the issue, informs The Kid that she is ashamed of his disgraceful conduct, but if he learned anything then this was the end of it.

My Aunt Martha. If this was the end of it then why did he have Mamie Epperson's poems to memorize? Jeez, he'd be wasting the entire year memorizing those darned poems, reciting out loud to the old lady with Dracula hiding behind the drapes waiting to sneak a little nip out of his neck. Didn't Ma realize that his life wasn't worth a plug nickel every time he walked through Miss Epperson's front door.

"Are you listening to me?"

"Yes Ma."

"Now get upstairs and memorize the first poem Mrs. Epperson marked for you."

"Yes Ma'am."

The Kid lay down and began reading:

Deal with another as you'd have another deal with you:
What you're unwilling to receive, Be sure you never do.

The Kid figured he didn't have to memorize the poem to know what Ma, courtesy Mamie Epperson, was driving at. Ma always had a point. Sure, being fair he understood, but maybe him thinking Pete Benson was an enemy had something to do with it too. Not only had he misjudged Pete Benson as some kind of bad guy, he pulled a dirty trick on the local Republican vote getter for something he didn't really understand. Didn't know a hoot about politics. Didn't care much either.

Ma claimed everybody, no matter how misguided, had the responsibility to vote and no twerp had the right to interfere with their rights. This wasn't Russia, Ma said. The Kid didn't understand that even though he had heard Ma go on about how no self-respecting American would buy the garbage handed out by the communists and fascists whoever they were.

Now that Ma had straightened him out, The Kid felt kinda sorry for Pete Benson. Shoot fire, everybody knew there would never be another Republican president. Ma said so.

THE BOYS

When the neighbors asked after Sis it was always with a smile and a word of praise because Miss Terrific is smart and a comfort to Ma. That's exactly what they tell Ma: "My, Helen must be a comfort to you." Ma's face would beam, and she'd about bust her buttons. She knows the truth when she hears it and talking about Sis makes her proud. And when the neighbors asked about Bobby Ma tells them what a treasure he is, and they all smile and agree with her.

But when the subject of Bud and Jack arrives the neighbors roll their eyes and the conversation turns to less sensitive subjects. They call them, "The Boys," or more formally, William and John, as if their proper names will somehow provide Ma an absolution of sorts. To Ma, they are Buddy and Jacky, and to their running mates they are Prunes and Red. It isn't that Ma suspects them of being crooks or smugglers or thieves or worse, but they have a way of getting into devilment that tests her resolve to speak only good things about her twosome.

Every neighbor within the confines of the East End know The Boys and the slick articles they run with –- Swede, Mex, Sarge, Soup, Cully to mame a few –- but cunning minds and fast feet have, so far, evaded the watchful eyes of the law. Oh they don't consort with Blackie Cole, the bootlegger who lives up on the bluff. According to Ma the malcontents who run with Blackie are pretty bad ones headed straight for damnation. Ma preaches on the evils of demon rum and paints a mighty bleak picture lest The Boys be tempted to mingle with one Blackie Cole or, worse yet, taste the devil's brew.

The point is that Ma has her hands full trying to keep ahead of the plotting and planning of her darlings, Buddy and Jacky. When one misses the ball the other one swats a home run. Idea wise, that is.

One time Prunes and Red were spotted by Mamie Epperson misappropriating -- a fifty-cent word for stealing -- some apples from her orchard a couple blocks away on 5th Avenue. Hearing her shout they hightailed it for home, rushed up stairs and changed their shirts. Mamie, an oldie whose long distance vision wasn't exactly up to snuff approached Ma asserting that The Boys had been taking her apples without permission. Ma called her precious sons down to face their accuser. Shame-faced Mamie said, "No, the rascals I saw wore different shirts." Ma just shook her head.

The neighbors generally put The Boys in the same pot, as if they were twins. Maybe because they were only a year plus apart in age had something to do with it, but they were as different as night and day.

Buddy was the eldest by a year, dark hair, quiet-like, a thinker, and in his younger days a fighter. By the time he had passed through eighth grade he had cleaned up on most of the East End toughs for this or that slur against the family name. Besides being good with his dukes, he was an idea guy who had a natural flair for making things. As far as The Kid was concerned, Prunes was bound to invent something truly grand that would enlighten the world.

One time when he was maybe fifteen Ma observes the chimney is about to topple down, the mortar having eroded due to the ravages of zero plus winters. So she enlists Buddy. He climbs a ladder to the eaves, shinnies up to the chimney and proceeds to build a scaffold around the chimney. Using his brain cells of which he has more than a few, he mixes the mortar and carefully cements the bricks together. All of this goes on under the eyes of Ma who, standing on the ground like a Top Sarge, has a more then a few suggestions about how to do the job. Digging his toes into the shingles for fear of falling off, the thought enters Buddy's skull that the last thing he requires is Ma's management style, but being a dutiful son he shuts his trap and completes the job with the skill of a master mason.

Anyway, while Prunes was in the basement working away on some project that would set the world on fire, Red was on the prowl seeking more victims who would fall under the spell of his charm. Flaming red hair, a princely smile and a shrewd mind gave Red the edge in any confrontation, adult or teenager. He could also run like the wind, vault with the best and had an intuition where danger to his precious body existed.

Red was a people person, always with a joke and a laugh, and was a teller of stories. When The Kid was a short pants buster he would stand at the kitchen window when Red went off to school, laughing as Red played the goof, like bumping into a tree and half-falling down. *Red waved and smiled until he disappeared around the corner. The Kid wondered who made Red feel better when he was downcast, but he never figured that one out. It was enough for him just to have Red around when his sky was filled with black clouds.*

Early on, Ma learned that she had a special cross to bear. One Sunday evening after supper Ma's out watering the garden and along comes Mr. Charlesworth on his evening stroll. Since the hose didn't have a cut off she walked back to the house to turn off the faucet. Returning to Mr. Charlesworth she chatted away about this and that, as pleasant as can be, but neither Ma nor Mr. Charlesworth saw The Boys lurking around the side of our house. When they spot Ma pointing the hose directly at Mr. Charlesworth a bright light marked, "IDEA," springs into their cunning minds. The water faucet is situated so that the elm tree in the backyard is between The Boys and Ma. Get the picture? Prunes and Red sure did.

One minute Ma is having this neighborly conversation and the next minute Mr. Charlesworth is getting a regular dousing. Ma is so stunned that she just keeps the hose aimed at Mr. Charlesworth, him sputtering and all. While all this is happening, The Boys put 'er in high gear and beat a retreat, laughing and having a merry old time, congratulating each other for being such quick thinkers.

Finally Ma drops the hose and starts apologizing with all the sincerity the good Lord gave her. Mr. Charlesworth stands there soaked from head to toe. Ma tries to regain her composure but knows she will be the laughing stock of the East End. A straight-laced Englishman, Mr. Charlesworth is the essence of politeness and courtesy, but his good form is sorely tested. He excuses himself, "under the circumstances," and sloshes on home. A trail of water follows him. Ma shouts after him that it is all her fault because the hose is old and seems to have a mind of its own turning on and off like that. But she knows better. So does Mr. Charlesworth.

From the back porch The Kid observes the episode, sees Red and Prunes disappear around the house like two Jesse Owens running the hundred yard dash. There wasn't any doubt in his mind who the culprits were. And there wasn't any question in Ma's mind, either. She had them pegged before they dropped out of sight.

As soon as Mr. Charlesworth gets out of earshot, Ma spies The Kid and yells, "Where are they?" Ma never ever says, "The Boys," because every time she hears those words it means that the wastrels are in some kind of fix, and some neighbor is after their hides. Being the fixer, Ma has to bail them out -- well, what she does actually is lie to protect the family name.

Bent over laughing, The Kid asks, "Who?" which was about as dumb as The Kid ever gets. Should have known Ma wasn't in any laughing mood. Ma points to the attic and orders The Kid to bed.

Ma lets out a tremendous, "YOU HOO," that thunders throughout the neighborhood. You gotta understand one thing. Ma's "YOU HOO," is one of the great calls to order of all time. Under normal circumstances she merely stands on the front porch or back porch, and her, "YOU HOO," summons the brood home forthwith. During the winter her, "YOU HOO," penetrates right through brick walls, and in the summer her yell rips the leaves off trees, down to the river up and over the bluff. Nothing stops her call to attention.

Everybody in the neighborhood could tell when Ma was simply calling the brood for supper or whether one of her offspring was in trouble. Now her, "YOU HOO," held a threat to life in it. The Boys were on the hot seat, no doubt about it, and it made the neighbors grin. Not being too bright, Buddy and Jacky ignored the booming command. It isn't dark yet, and their lively minds were still working furiously. Not smartly, just furiously.

The rules Ma set, there was no other law east of the Mississippi, decreed that the only thing young boys could get into after dark was, "divelment." To Ma, sunlight protected her brood from getting into trouble, and when the sun disappeared trouble with a capital "T" abounded. There was no option, no relief, no pleading, no nothing. Rules were rules.

With The Boys safely tucked in and nobody in authority knocking at the door, Ma could rest easily, her place in society preserved for another day. But on this Sunday evening she had YOU HOOed 'til her voice cracked. Her command had not been respected, and to Ma, that was unforgivable.

The Boys wander in the back door with plenty of daylight to spare, figuring their early return would prove to Ma how much they loved her. She wasn't buying. She had Prunes and Red up against the wall, blasting away like a number ten howitzer. The Kid tunes in his ears, listens to the stupids wimp their way around Ma's wrath. "Gee, Ma, we wouldn't be dumb enough to turn on the hose."

This comes from Red who, The Kid smirks, knows is exactly dumb enough to do just that.

"Ma, we need a new hose," declares Buddy.

"We sure know he is the fairest guy alive," says Jacky.

Ma listens to this drivel and orders them to apologize to the poor man. The Boys consider an apology an admission of guilt, so they wimp away some more, their hole getting deeper all the time.

"Which one of you turned on the faucet?"

Nose to nose they turn on each other accusing eyes ready to blame the other. Fortunately reason wins out. They understand that if they do not face their doom together, they are forever lost. Slinking out the door, The Boys leave for Mr. Charlesworth's house.

"And what are you still doing up young man?"

The Kid knows suddenly that he isn't the only dumb cluck in Ma's brood. At this rate it is going to be a long summer.

Next day The Kid wanders down the alley to Russ's Texaco station thinking the busters might have a game of kick the can or hide and go seek after supper when it starts to cool off. He shoots an imaginary ball through the hoop attached to Johnny's garage, swishes it perfectly. Last fall he was All-Alley, scored forty-eight points in an all-day basketball game. Whoever had the idea for alleys must have been a genius, so thought The Kid.

Phew, it was hot. He ambled on doing a little of this and a little of that, but if the truth be known, not much of anything. Russ was working on some bohunk's car, a 1928 Something-Or-Other which had seen better days. Russ pulls the plugs and tells the guy that he needs new ones, but the guy ain't buying. Says that the plugs are original equipment, and they seem just dandy to him, so why doesn't Russ just clean 'em up. Russ explains that the plugs have ceased life and aren't worth a hoot and until they are replaced with new ones the sodbuster's car will stutter along just as always.

Russ receives a blank stare and knows his sales pitch went west. Mutters a lot when he tries to gap the suckers that haven't any gap left in them. The Kid watches the miser drive down 4th avenue, his 1928 loser a clunking and bucking and laying down a cloud of smoke. Russ's eyes get a mean look, but out of respect for The Kid's age he keeps his own blue fumes down to a mutter. "Can you believe that son-of-a ...," Russ sputters.

The Kid likes Russ, always has a good word and a smile and is the best darned mechanic in the East End. On his really good days Russ allows The Kid to select a soda pop for free. The Kid is now eyeing the soda box filled with ice for the day's customers. Likes cream soda best, but it's always a challenge for him when Russ tells him to take one. When that happens The Kid opens the lid and stares at all the bottles, and after a zillion years finally takes out a cream soda that is what he was going to take all along. But it's morning now and Russ isn't in the best of moods having lost to the bohunk in the 1928 Something-Or-Other, so with his prospects of a free soda dashed, The Kid meanders on home thinking about nothing at all.

With a glass of Kool-Aid in his hand and sitting on the back porch swing, The Kid is about to listen to the Cubs game. Ma's bungalow has a big front porch where you can sit and take in the neighborhood goings-on, but The Kid likes the back porch. A huge elm tree shading the backyard makes the afternoon just Jim Dandy.

Red is busy in the backyard putting a new tire on his bike. Hunkered down on his haunches, Red is content, likes to work on his bike, which, by the way, needs lots of work. His bike wasn't much to look at being made from parts foraged from unsuspecting East End victims. Once Prunes blabbed to The Kid that he would stand lookout when Red appropriated a needed part from a bicycle whose ownership was less than positive. The Kid hadn't just fallen off a turnip truck. He knows what Prunes means.

But tires are tough to come by. Red's tires were plain skinny, the kind people had before some brilliant guy invented balloon tires. Red's tires are so full of rubber band patches there is hardly any tire remaining at all, just one patch after another stemming the tide, or in this case the air.

Red has a paper route that brings in hard earned coins, and he saves up his pennies and nickels and dimes until he has the price of a tire. With his new tire firmly pumped up, Red whistles a tune and adjusts the spokes so the wheel runs true, a happy guy at peace in the back yard.

Getting somewhat bored eying Red tune up the old bike, The Kid wanders down to the basement. Prunes is hard at work on a pair of skis he found discarded in the dump. The front curved sections were splintered and Prunes was deep in thought figuring out how to fix the damage. When Prunes is in a thinking mood he ain't about to talk to a little squirt, so The Kid skedaddles back to the porch and gets set for the ball game.

As Red is tightening the nuts on the front wheel, Prunes waltzes into the backyard carrying an axe and two blocks of wood. Prunes' plans call for fashioning curved supports for the skis, but when he spots Red he walks over to see the new tire. Holding the axe over the tire, Prunes jokes about what would happen if he drops it. Red looks at Prunes like he is some kind of nitwit. Fact is that's what Red calls him.

Prunes is about to reply, but at that moment he loses his grip and the axe falls straight down on Red's new tire. With a sploosh the tire unwraps itself, and with a thud drops to the turf. Red's tire lays on the ground imitating a garter snake gone to heaven.

Time, as they say, stands still. Transfixed, Prunes stares at his offending hand praying his feet will get him somewhere else. Red's mouth hangs open. He picks up the lifeless tire and puts the ends together hoping for a miracle that will magically make the tire whole again. Watching Prunes and Red facing each other, The Kid's throat dries up. The storm is about to pop.

"Jeez, Red, I didn't mean to do it," Prunes whimpers.

Red picks up the axe and takes off after Prunes hollering that he's gonna plant the axe in Prunes worthless skull. The Kid yelps for Ma and she comes running. When The Kid explains that Red is about to slice Prunes into little pieces, Ma tears into the backyard. First Prunes speeds around the house, then comes Red swearing up a storm.

Normally Prunes is of a mind to defend himself from anyone, including Red who he has by size and fighting experience, but now he's one pale-faced cookie running for his life. Red is forever the guy with a ready smile and a line a mile long, but when the occasion arises he has the fiercest temper of Ma's brood.

Finally Ma collars Red and grabs the axe. Gasping and wheezing, Prunes promises that if it takes him his entire days on earth he will buy Red a new tire. The Kid never saw Prunes so contrite. Maybe it's just raw fear, but The Kid knows sincerity when he hears it. Red points his finger at the offender and hollers that Prunes'll never live long enough to buy him a new tire.

"Dammit to hell," Red sputters.

Ma orders Prunes straight away to the basement that is hardly a punishment because that's where Prunes wants to go anyway. Then she puts an arm around Red and quiets him down, forgets Red's profanity that is just as well considering the circumstances. The Kid catches a glimpse of Red's eyes and doesn't like what he sees, knows this isn't the end of it.

For the next few weeks Ma's bungalow is a mighty gloomy place. Each morning Red departs early and joins up with the rat pack. Prunes stays put in the basement, losing his-self in the ski project. After designing the support pieces to fit exactly the curvature of the front ends, he glues the pieces into position and drills holes from the bottom of the ski into the support pieces. The Kid watches him countersink the holes just so, and after twisting in the screws Prunes fills the screw heads with bees wax. It was a mighty fine job of work, indeed.

Prunes displays his handy work at supper and tells Ma how he intends setting all kinds of ski jump records. Red agrees, not a whiff of sarcasm in his voice.

The Boys have an understanding, so The Kid thinks. But Red looks upon Prunes' skis as an opportunity to gain revenge. One bright day when Prunes absents himself from the old homestead Red sneaks down to the basement. Red isn't any wood worker, but he is clever. Careful like, he digs out the beeswax and twists out the screws. Then Red fills the holes up with nothing but bees wax. The only thing holding the ski ends together was glue. His job of flimflammery is as slick as can be. All Red has to do is wait for winter.

Buddy's absence came about when, desperate for cash, he peddled his bike on a gravel road out past the airport to pick onions at ten cents a bushel. Problem was the onions awaiting him were thumb-sized and it took all day of back-breaking work in the hot sun to fill two bushel baskets -- total earnings of twenty cents. After peddling home he was one disgusted buster. No matter how much he needed cash, he vowed his onion topping days were over.

To all outward appearances Jack is over his mad and The Boys are back together again, plotting and planning and running free with their buddies, making life hell for anybody stupid enough to draw their attention. But Ma's rules and regulations are firmly in place as God had intended. In before dark was inviolate -- all that "divelment" was waiting out there someplace to corrupt the family. Well, really, The Boys. Ma knew Buddy and Jacky were particularly susceptible to corruption. She had The Kid well in hand, and in Ma's eyes Sis was pure as the driven snow. But The Boys were getting older and their pals, the Neanderthals, all stayed out after the sun dropped over the yardarm. Independence lurked in The Boy's hearts, a skulking beast that thumbed its nose at rules and regulations. Something had to be done.

The attic had been turned into sleeping quarters for The Boys and The Kid. Each had a bed in a dormer. Each dormer had three small windows that fronted onto the roof. A slanted ledge maybe eighteen inches wide made any attempt to leave the dormer a precarious deed. At Red's suggestion Prunes tried to climb down, but he darned near fell off. So Red wisely decided they had to come up with a something to accomplish an escape. Prunes thought about the problem and Red watched him closely, waiting for an inspiration from his older brother. As often happened, Prunes was inspired.

While Prunes assumes the post of lookout, Red appropriates fifty feet of rope from some unsuspecting pigeon that, he claims, will never miss it. While Red makes certain Ma's out of sight, Prunes makes a rope ladder that they hide in a storage closet in the attic. Sick and tired of being YOU HOOed home when the sun reached the horizon, The Boys are primed to taste their freedom.

Problem is they can climb down easily but they can't get over the edge of the roof on the way up. Returning home after their first night's adventure they find out it's impossible to make it over the ledge. Trapped outside with nowhere to go, the evening's fun takes on a sinister meaning. Disaster faces them. But, Red, that sly devil, figures it out.

He gets atop the back porch railing, and with a boost from Prunes climbs up on the flat roof. Reaching back down Red grabs Prunes hand and jerks him up. It ain't much of a job to lift themselves onto the slanted roof of the house, and from there they creep on hands and knees to the dormer. Which presents the tricky part. With only eighteen inches of a sharply slanted roof to work with they glance at the ground, gulp, and dig their fingers into the roof. They make their way inch by inch to the dormer window and safety. Once inside Prunes pulls up the useless rope ladder, a great downer but decidedly a bust as an upper. They lay in bed discussing the risk. One misstep and it is curtains, but without risk, Red says nothing is won. Prunes agrees, says he'd rather miss dinner than miss out on the night games which is a huge admission taking in Prunes addiction to vittles three times a day. So began The Boys nightly outings.

One thing the bozos never noticed was the tomatoes Ma put on the back porch railing to ripen. Her tomatoes rested precisely in the spot where they stepped on the railing to begin their evening climb. Each morning when Ma inspects the tomatoes she is puzzled why the darned things are smashed or lying on the ground. She just can't understand it. Ma is quick to the mark, no doubt about that, but even her reasoning power is fallible once in a while. The smashed tomatoes never did lead to her discovery of The Boys nighttime capers.

The Kid decides that Ma's rules are meant for males only

because she bends them all over the place for Sis. Of course, Sis is the oldest and the trustworthy one of the brood and has a whole lot more influence with Ma than The Boys. And Sis has a summer job that brings in cold hard cash Ma never thought she'd ever see again.

Anyway, Sis is allowed to date and not have to be home before darkness falls. The Kid supposes that was fair on Ma's part because Sis wouldn't have seen many shows unless Ma raised her sun over the yardarm ban. When he thinks about it, which ain't too often, The Kid allows as to how Ma has an inherent distrust of The Boys. And he is absolutely right.

One balmy evening when Sis is motoring home from a downtown movie with one of the neighborhood boys she dated, she spots Prunes and Red hamming it up with the local pack. Sis waves to them and gives them a "Hi." The dummies wave back, but they go right on playing, plotting or planning or whatever, never suspecting their nights of freedom are numbered.

When Sis gets home she asks Ma, "Where are Bud and Jack?"

"Why do you ask," Ma questions.

"Because I just saw them down by Belgium village," Sis replies all sweet and helpful like.

"Can't be," Ma says.

"My eyes are twenty-twenty," Sis responds, "And I saw them clearly."

Ma informs Sis that The Boys arrived home tired as all get out and were upstairs in bed asleep like they were supposed to be and why did Sis make such a foolish statement. Well Sis says, The Boys didn't look sleepy to her. Which tears it for Prunes and Red.

Among Ma's curious habits is that when she checks the house at night she carries an alarm clock with her. Never a flashlight or a club, but that darned old alarm clock. Probably wanted to prove what time it was should she confront some thief after her cash supply. Her nocturnal wanderings were known to one and all, she made her rounds to the tick-tock of her trusty alarm. So up to the attic Ma prances and finds no Buddy, no Jacky. Sis's story proves right on the mark, which Ma takes as a personal affront. She sits there in the dark holding onto her old alarm clock waiting for the princes of darkness, wondering how to approach this latest crisis.

Later, much, much later, The Boys come a sneaking along the roof, pause at the dangerous part, the slanted roof fronting the dormer, then inch slowly to the windows. Red is in the lead, but after disengaging the hooks holding the screen he hears the dreaded tick-tock of Ma's alarm clock. Red may be foolish, but no fool. Slowly he backs away from the window frame and allows as to how his dearest brother, good old Prunes, can have the honor of entering first. Red says he'd be only too happy to attach the screen after his big brother is safely inside. Prunes likes Red's attitude and is about half-way through the window when Ma yells:

"YOU BOYS GET IN HERE."

Prunes leaps backwards, nearly takes Red and himself off the roof. Hanging by their thumbs, the miscreants have no place to go but in. Shaking with fear inside they go.

"WHERE HAVE YOU BEEN?"

Red starts to tell her how this voice called them to go out and save the neighborhood from Blackie Cole's gang or some such rot. Prunes nods his head in agreement, but Ma freezes them with a Laser-bolt stare she developed long before Superman entered The Kid's domain.

Ma says she is so disgusted she's beside herself that The Kid thinks is darned hard to do even for Ma. She declares the entire East End will know what a couple of no-accounts she has to raise. "What will become of you?" Ma moans. Shaking her head she orders them to bed. And with a parting shot she roars:

"I'LL DEAL WITH YOU IN THE MORNING."

Prunes and Red jump into bed straight away. Petrified, they

stew all night long, toss and turn, praying for forgiveness. What is Ma going to do to them? They had violated one of Ma's most important rules: THOU SHALL NOT STAY OUT AFTER DARK.

It is a somber breakfast table. Having squealed on them, Sis is feeling pangs of conscience. She sits quiet as a mouse as The Boys are about to walk the plank. All ears, The Kid is waiting for the gavel to bring the court to order. Ma's not saying beans, nothing at all, which is a surprise because Ma always takes the floor when something important is on tap. Prunes and Red are at that eating age, but the old Adams-apples can hardly pass the food down. This was one morning when Ma's oatmeal not only stuck to their ribs, but in their throats as well.

Having her fill of silence Ma begins to speak, straight out, no namby-pamby. Says she was awake all night long pondering what to do, asking God for guidance. Red groans, knows he's doomed. Ma shoots him her lasers that tend to freeze a guy in place. Prunes and Red straighten up and give her their rapt attention that is an achievement since both were born shy on attention giving. The Kid is enjoying the scene because if he'd been told once he'd been told a zillion times to sit up straight and take it like a man.

"I've decided that from now on you boys can stay out until ten o'clock."

Sharp intake of breath, disbelief hover in their eyes. Is Ma really saying this? Here they expected to be grounded for the next millennium and Ma is allowing them to stay out *after* dark. Ten o'clock. Unbelievable.

"But at ten o'clock the doors and windows will be locked, rain, cold, hot, summer or winter. And there will be no more climbing up on the roof."

Ma says serious-like that she is placing her trust in them, that if they bring shame to the family name or get into real trouble, she doesn't know what she will do. Ma's good at the sympathy business and has the good cop bad cop routine down pat.

The Boys are smart enough not to lay their undying thanks on too thick, and Ma knows she doesn't have to worry about them all that much. They weren't smugglers nor thieves or rumrunners, just a couple of "divels" that had to be watched.

The Kid figures Ma was pretty darned smart. If she had denied them what their friend's parents allowed, she could wind up with a more serious problem. And, come to think of it, she saved half the tomato crop, too.

It was a real buster of a summer, humidity hung on The Kid's shoulders like a steamy blanket. To get a bit of relief from the steaming attic Ma allowed The Kid sleep on the front porch, but when he awoke the fog coming up from the Mississippi promised another sweltering day. The Kid had visions of the picture show downtown that advertised its air conditioning -- "COOL, COOL, COOL" -- but he didn't have the price of admission. One thin dime was what he needed, but didn't have. The Kid considered asking Ma for a couple of nickels, but knows better. Probably get a lecture about suffering, and how it was good for the soul. From what Ma said about hell and damnation The Kid decided he better lead an upright life, but the possibility of the hereafter down below couldn't be any worse than it was right now.

No matter how slowly The Kid navigated along, he was wet with sweat. Kinda took the stuffings out of his daytime excursions. He lolled around Russ's station, but nothing exciting was going on. Even Russ had slowed down, sat at his grimy desk complaining about the weather. When a car putt-putts in for gas, Russ muttered a hopeful "fill 'er up," but his heart ain't in it. Brother, it was hot.

With nothing to do and no place to go The Kid pokes along up the alley, catches sight of some activity in Swede's shack. Nothing but a crummy garage that has a northeast list to it, it is the headquarters for the East End wastrels led by Prunes and

Red. Forbidden territory for The Kid, but what the hey, Red says if you're scared to take a risk you'll never get anything you want. Like a mouse testing its whiskers for danger, The Kid wanders in, finds the Neanderthals in deep discussion.

He adopts a slouch against the far wall and takes in the atmosphere. That is, if you call a thick pall of smoke hanging listlessly about the shack, the emissions from a pack of Twenty Grand cigarettes, and the stale smell of beer atmosphere. Odds and ends of food, lifted no doubt from some unsuspecting merchant, lay scattered on the floor. The gang's headquarters had never smelled nor looked better.

The wisenheimers were planning their day's activity involving hopping a freight to Barstow, a switching yard about twenty miles away. There were six or seven bodies talking at once, but it seemed to The Kid that Prunes, Red and Swede were the main actors. As he took in the sights and smells of the shack, The Kid decides a little outing in the clean rural air would do a lot for them mentally. Sort of clean out their respective brains that badly needed airing.

The band of merry men laid out their battle plans, most of which had to do with outwitting the railroad coppers. Because of his hair, Red was the target of every railroad dick east of the Mississippi. Trains obsessed Red. From the time he was a little shaver Red dreamed of being a train engineer. Once when he was about ten or eleven he sneaked up into the cab of an engine that was idling in the station downtown, intending to drive that sucker to Chicago. Red had his hand on the throttle ready to chug that son-of-a-gun on its way when he was discovered. The engineer and fireman start yelling and waving their oil cans, and with the railroad copper they begin chasing the red-haired kid. Never had a chance. Red bugs out the far side of the cab and was last seen high-tailing it toward the East End.

It was a close call for Red, but not close enough to deter him from his constant dream -- the thrill of railroading. He takes to disguising himself by wearing various stocking caps to cover his hair, but after years of confrontations and his pitiful attempts at disguise the railroad coppers whoop it up at the first sight of the hooded marvel. Red's finding it more and more difficult to ride the rails, but with a devious mind and a determined body, the coppers haven't a chance. None of the Neanderthals consider Red a liability. The blues are so busy shagging Red the rest of the crew disappear amid all the yelling and chasing.

So here they are planning a quick trip out to Barstow where they'll drop off and pick up a freight hauling coal for the return trip. The object of this adventure is to kick off coal when the freight passes through the East End, then when the freight slows entering downtown the merry band'll drop off and hitchhike back to the East End where the precious clumps of coal lay beside the tracks.

It dawns on The Kid where Swede was going last week when he saw him trudging up the alley with a dirty old gunny sack over his shoulder. All of this effort, hopping the freight to Barstow and all that, would end up filling the ancient stove sitting in Swede's shack. Which was interesting, but to The Kid didn't seem like that much of an adventure. The Kid skedaddles off to find his running mates. At least they talked in complete sentences.

Ma found out everything The Boys did, a truth obvious to everybody but The Boys. The Kid figures that the adult world has some sort of secret communication system that is in place solely to obstruct the adventures and all-around good times of their respective offspring. In any event, Ma knows of the latest escapades involving The Boys and the Rock Island railroad.

One particularly hot evening, the brood is eating supper, all seated at the kitchen table like they are supposed to be. Like the weather, the conversation drags. Ma's inquiry into the day's activities seemed benevolent, no big deal, until she starts lecturing about the dangers of hopping freights and how everyone she had heard about who was devoted to this sort of pastime had either lost their legs in some tragic accident or been arrested and thrown in jail and never heard from again as agitating the railroad authorities was such a serious crime and all, and how she would hate to think that anyone she KNEW was stupid enough to go jumping on and off speeding trains, and if she found about such goings-on she wouldn't be able to sleep at nights.

"Don't you think so, boys?" Said sweetly.

The Boys nodded their heads as if to say, "Yes, Ma you are perfectly right." Shifty looks from the coal dust twins bring about a momentary silence at the table.

Ma persists. She wasn't about to be dismissed by a couple of adolescents who were not PROPERLY listening to her. As Ma becomes more animated, The Boys become more somber. Protesting that they were hanging on her every word, The Boys vow they wouldn't be caught dead hopping freights.

Which was not the most encouraging thought Ma expected to hear. So on and on she plows. The Boys are using the Rock Island for a high old time, she says. If worse comes to worse she will be the one who will have to extract their worthless hides from some jail cell.

The Boys know Ma will protect them right or wrong before anybody, any time. She has defended the two wise guys through all their escapades, but once the confrontation with school Marms or neighbors or merchants was over with Ma dealt out her own punishment.

Ma declares that if anybody at HER table does anything on the far side of the law they, "have to pay the piper." Ma, however, is the piper and if you missed that bit of household wisdom you had to be really brain damaged. Fortunately they had quick minds and fast feet. If they were caught, and this was a big if, Ma never heard about it.

Listening to Ma giving The Boys a right smart what for The

Kid concluded that life on the open road was over for Prunes and Red. After supper he spots Mr. Downing weeding his garden and walks across the alley to talk to him. Mr. Downing was a huge man, especially so to a little guy, but he spoke softly and somehow reassuring even when he talked about things The Kid knew nothing about. Hearing the waa, waaa, waaaa of a freight, Mr. Downing pulls out his gold railroad watch and checks the time.

"Two-O-Five is a minute late, Bobby."

The Kid nods, respecting Mr. Downing's opinion on anything as important as a train being on time. Shifting from foot to foot, The Kid wonders if he ought to ask Mr. Downing about how dangerous hopping freights could be.

"Something you wanted to ask, Bobby?"

The Kid changes gears, thinks asking about the danger in riding the rails wasn't the smart thing to do. Not after Ma's talk at the supper table. So he shakes his head no, and tells Mr. Downing that he'd better get on home because Ma is expecting him. The train engineer smiles, chuckling as The Kid shuffles home.

Sitting on the back porch swing in the fading light, The Kid can still see Mr. Downing, hoe in hand jabbing at his garden. Mr. Downing is a right good man, but it doesn't take a brick to fall on his head to realize it was the train engineer who ratted on Prunes and Red. He didn't like what he was thinking, but maybe Mr. Downing told Ma in order to save The Boys from a long-term prison sentence. Brother, this was a real problem. Knowing what was right and what was wrong could give a guy a headache.

"What are you thinking about, Bobby?"

"Nothing, Ma, nothing at all."

Ma disappears into the kitchen still doing some task or other. The Kid decides that she has her work cut out for her when she goes toe to toe with Prunes and Red, a matched pair whose collective brains were about the most devious recorded in all mankind, a pair who could outfox anybody, anywhere, anytime.

Except Ma.

MCKINLEY

The Kid stood below the bluff staring up apprehensively at the forbidding redbrick school that was to be his new home away from home -- McKinley Elementary School. Helen and Bud and Red had preceded him setting all kinds of standards for studies, behavior and all-around conduct. Well, actually, Sis had set the standards being smart, and well behaved and a pleasure to Ma. With Sis, the teachers probably thought Ma was raising the best and the brightest in the whole East End, but then Prunes and Red show up and they prove that when the family genes get scrambled just about anything that can go wrong does go wrong.

Being the anointed defender of the family name Prunes was more than willing to clean house on any tough stupid enough to test him. The schoolyard had more than one tornado of flying bodies with Prunes freewheeling fists in the eye of the fight. Meanwhile Red is giving the teachers his best toothy smile and a line a mile long that reduced McKinley's educational process to its zero option. When Red graduated he left the teachers wondering what in the name of Lucifer had happened to them. Less said about Red, the better.

As The Kid shuffled up the concrete steps McKinley's teaching corps awaited another one of Ma's offspring with anticipation -- or, maybe not.

Seemed there were a zillion half-formed bodies coming from every direction. Already he missed the one-room gray clapboard school where everybody knew everybody. His enthusiasm ran dry, just a bug-eyed, open-mouthed poor excuse that once had been a big fish in a little pond. The Kid searched intently for the old familiar faces, but so far he had only spotted Mary Lou. She of Grennel's star wars fame charged up the steps like Teddy Roosevelt leading his troops up San Juan Hill. Frightening.

Without a friendly face to rely on, The Kid swallows his anxiety and greets Mary Lou as nice as you please. She comes to a stop, staring at The Kid, wondering if he still was the brain damaged no account she had buried in the minor leagues. ML produces a superior smile, going on about how her mother had tutored her all summer long and that she's mighty well prepared to meet any challenge McKinley could possibly offer, wonders sweetly if he'll be capable of matching her wits.

The Kid lets all this drivel drift in one ear and out the other, produces a mutter that contained a damn or two. ML gives off with one of her straight-laced frowns, complaining about him swearing in front of girls and if the teachers were aware of his foul mouth wouldn't that be a shame?

The Kid knows he stepped in it, figures that sooner rather than later ML will inform this or that teacher of the disgusting habits of the dimwitted boy students McKinley had inherited from Grennel.

ML prances through the huge front doors like she owns the place. The Kid follows slowly wishing he had enough sense to keep his big trap shut. But on second thought, he decides he ain't gonna let Mary Lou cast the evil eye on his first day in the big time. And sitting there in his homeroom pretty as you please were Davey and Hooter, Duffy and the Cage, Johnny and the H, and Icky. Icky? The Kid thought Icky had moved out of town, but there he sat, slumped down in his seat, eyes staring at the floor. Icky ain't the best looking guy by far. Had some mighty peculiar looking skin, all blotchy-like. When they were in kindergarten Icky sat next to The Kid. The Kid remembered well, wished he didn't.

Their teacher back then, Miss Buler, had a thing about birthdays, and birthday parties -- probably some rite of passage for kindergarten busters. Anyway, the ordained birthday kid would bring a treat, something like cup cakes with frosting spread across the tops, and the entire class would sit in a circle while the birthday boy or girl tossed out the cup cakes or whatever. Then in a wail of squeaky voices the class would sing happy birthday while the dimwit birthday kid sat embarrassed wishing the event of the day was over with. Miss Buler got a charge out of the affair because her voice raised an octave if the object of all the attention did not thank everybody properly for the cup cakes this or that mother had stayed up all night baking for their pleasure.

So its Icky's birthday, and he brings in a whole basket full of nicely frosted cup cakes that The Kid and some other busters finger appropriately before the celebration. Miss Buler gathers the class in the obligatory circle on the floor, and Icky looking every which way stumbles around dropping the cakes into expectant hands. It happens that Icky is sitting on the hardwood next to The Kid and his blotchy face by now has turned a crimson hue that makes him look worse than ever. Miss Buler gives the downbeat, and with everybody staring at Icky the happy birthday song begins.

All of a sudden The Kid feels a watery substance sluicing against his leg and with a yelp he leaps to his feet. In all the excitement that simple-minded Icky peed his pants and is staring at the far wall wishing he was spacing out on another planet.

Miss Buler is about to give The Kid a bashing when she spies the golden stream Icky had bestowed on his classmate. Well sir, there is a couple of screams and a general all-around retreat, a pull-back you might say from the Icky sitting there with his mind orbiting the rings of Saturn. The circle ain't any circle no more.

Miss Buler attempts to restore order and deal with Icky at the same time. Muttering, "Will you look at that," she puts an arm hold on Icky and marches him to the restroom. With a withering look she dares anybody to make a move. The busters freeze.

Poor old Icky won't come out of the toilet, and Miss Buler who never says anything louder than a quiet, "shush," is yelling at the top of her voice, which in the halls of McKinley is no small happening. Best The Kid can remember Icky may have stayed secluded in the can the entire day. May have been there all these years for all The Kid knows.

Now he is sitting next to Icky once again in the big house they called McKinley, and wouldn't you know it but their teacher is none other than Miss Buler. When Icky sees her he about faints, and Davey Jackson and Duffy who have elephantine memories of Icky's never-to-be-forgotten watershed birthday know what his agitation is all about. Davey never did have the sense the good Lord gave him so at recess he sidles up to Icky and asks the poor bugger if he's still celebrating his birthdays like he did in the good old days. Icky stands there like a deaf mute staring out at the Mississippi, cursing the day he met up with Davey and The Kid and Duffy again.

The Kid throws a punch at Davey and gives Duffy a snappy what for. Duffy takes the hint and speaks up telling Icky that he don't have a worry in the world because they're a bunch of okay guys. Which isn't the first time Duffy lies, but a strange thing happens. Icky's orbs take in his tormentors full face on, and says thanks which for Icky is like reciting the Gettysburg address. It wasn't long after that Icky puts a complete sentence together, out loud so everybody can hear him. The Kid figures that they had done a bit of all right by Icky. Now all they had to do was find a cure for that ugly blotchy skin.

Although the whizzers spend most of their time assigned to Miss Buler, their homeroom teacher, they troop along to Miss Vance and Miss White and Miss I'm Brand New So Give Me A Break to imprint upon the rascals their own brands of teaching. Each brandishes a ruler or a finely cut switch when tempers got out of hand. Mr. Graves, however, needed no artificial assistance when it came to keeping the busters on the straight and narrow. The only male teacher at McKinley, Mr. Graves taught shop and gym, and as they say, he had seen it all. All the boys took shop. Probably because that was where they were headed.

Some guys had a knack for wood working, like Prunes who was a master. Then there were all-thumbers like The Kid who would put a four by four block of wood on the lathe, and if it was a good day, come out with a nicely formed toothpick. By gar, The Kid could make those wood chips fly. Problem was he didn't know what he was doing and never did get the hang of it. After a couple weeks of this foolishness, Mr. Graves says that everybody has to complete a project. Shoot fire, The Kid figures there goes all the fun, but what the hey, he'll just make this beauty of an end table pictured in one of shop magazines. Three burnished oak shelves in the shape of a half circle held together by three legs appeared just the ticket to The Kid.

Basically, Mr. Graves is a kindly man, and a helpful man. But he's getting a wee bit tired giving all this individual help to The Kid. Finally, he orders Hooter to help The Kid as he wasn't going to the hereafter waiting for the blister to catch onto simple directions. Furthermore, if he hears any more snickers about that, "bastard file," he'll send the wisenheimers home for good.

Day after day The Kid works on the end table of his dreams. After ruining piece after piece of solid oak, the H takes pity on him, cuts three shelves that, by golly, look just like the ones in the magazine. The Kid appraises the shelves and envisions Ma taking the finished product to her heart. But he has to admit that the shelves he is so puffed up about are the Hooter's work, not his. It wasn't that The Kid didn't try. It was simply a matter of talent. Of which he had none.

The Kid comforts himself with the thought that there are more important matters to consider than a stupid end table. His homeroom was divided into two semesters, the A group started their school life in September and the B group in January. Something about age, but how the authorities-that-be figured this system out was a puzzlement to The Kid. Only thing he knew for sure was that the A group was a half a year ahead of the busters that came from his old school with the steeple which, truth be told, he had nearly forgotten.

The Kid might have been making a hash out of his end table, but for Miss Buler and Miss Vance and Miss White he is doing a bit of all right. Mary Lou being her most obnoxious self explains away every problem known to mankind, but her antics don't faze him. Often as not Miss Buler ignored Mary Lou and picked out some other poor sap to produce an answer to the key question of the day, but The Kid would just as soon have Miss Encyclopedia be the jumping jack of all knowledge. It was safer that way.

Half way through the first semester Miss Buler announces that the annual spelling bee would be held next week. "The entire room," Miss Buler smiles grandly, "will participate."

Voice from the back of the room says, "A&B together?"

"I said the entire room, didn't I?"

On the way home The Kid spies Mary Lou surrounded by all these girl-type bootlickers with a zillion books in their paws asking their star performer to spell Madagascar or some such word he'd never heard of. Cripes, thinks The Kid, Miss Buler might just as well give the ML first prize and get the torture over with.

Davey, who has an eye for the obvious spots the bootlickers, gives him a poke, asks all innocent like, "Spell horse .... for me will ya Kid?"

"How about, 'bastard file,'" chimes in the Duffy.

"Why ya picking on me?" says The Kid, a bit miffed.

"Yer our one great hope," Says Davey as he motions to ML and her groupees.

"How about spelling end table," snickers Hooter.

"You mean endless table, don't ya," roars Duffy.

Are these guys serious? The thought that he is their great hope tumbles through The Kid's cranium, gets stuck in the part that suggests he is capable of defeating Miss Buler's shining star, the one and only champeeen, Mary Lou Johnson.

On the day of the spelling bee Miss Buler shows up in a new dress. Frilly thing, all the rage, but it loses its effect with her waving her yard stick at the busters who she knows will start laughing when some poor sap misses a word.

For once The Kid is serious, and as the god's decreed, he ends up facing ML in the finals. The big prize is a trip to Junior High to engage some other poor sap in a spell off. Ma thinks this would just about make her day so that's why The Kid is so serious.

"MASQUERADE," announces Miss Buler.

The Kid shuffles, tosses in an E where an A should have been. Knows immediately he had goofed.

"Incorrect." Groans. Yardstick posed, about to strike.

"Masquerade," intones ML. "M A S Q U E R A D E."

First darn word and down the drain he slides. The Kid returns to his seat, no longer the great hope of McKinley's male population. Worse yet, he catches sight of one of Mary Lou's superior grins. It was going to be a long semester.

As Miss Buler dismissed school for the day she points to The Kid. "I would like to see you, Bobby."

Jeez, what have I done now? tumbles through his thinker. Ma wouldn't give him the business for losing, probably give him the old saw about doing your best is what counts. Holy Smokers, it was just one lousy word. He tells himself to stand up tall like Ma would want, keeps his gazers on Miss Buler as she tidies her desk, stands the yardstick against the wall.

"How do you like school?"

Comes out pleasant like, but the undertow just might sink him. Except for that dratted table which by now was shrinking up to nothing, school ain't too bad. If the facts were known, he kinda likes school. Just prays that he don't have to lug home any notes, especially those bad news kind that Ma has to sign.

"Just fine, Miss Buler." Got it out first rate. None of that quivery lip stuff.

"Would you like to move to the A semester?"

The Kid is deep into confession, thinking about his recent record of misdeeds. Maybe blab about the crummy job he's doing in shop, or about giving Davey the answers to the math tests. No couldn't do that. Whoa! What in blazes did SHE SAY? MOVE TO THE A GROUP? The Kid has his mouth wide open, giving out the impression of Kenny Murchins who mumbles and slobbers and is a pitiful sight indeed.

Miss Buler hands him a note, offers a grade A teacher smile. "If your mother has no objection."

"Thanks, Miss Buler."

He is racing home double quick time when Davey and the gang nail him with questions fast as BBs shot from Hooter's air rifle.

"Ya in trouble? Mr. Graves give ya the old heave ho?"

"Nah," says The Kid. "See ya after supper." Darned if he'd rat out before he got to Ma. By gum, for once this is good news.

He is looking right direct at Ma when he delivers the note. She seems a wee bit apprehensive, which considering the notes she had received from McKinley's teaching fraternity about Buddy and Jacky were the Go to Jail kind.

But The Kid suspects the reason Ma hesitates is because some kindhearted parent, as in Mrs. Johnson, had already told her that Mary Lou had skunked the Kid in the spelling bee contest.

But one swipe at the message changes her attitude.

"This," yelps Ma, "is wonderful."

He gets a smackeroo and a hug that is about as good as it gets. The Kid figures Ma's life is on the upswing.

By this time the end table is taking on a life of it's own. Mr. Graves informs The Kid that he ought to be able to cut the legs without going through an entire lumberyard. Claims that it is a simple job, just three lousy pieces of equal length. The Kid gets the idea that when Mr. Graves uses the word simple, he is actually referring to him, but being a nice guy the teacher tries to spare The Kid's feelings. Whenever Mr. Graves passes The Kid's bench, he shrugs his shoulders and mutters a lot, tells H for the hundredth time to help The Kid. For crying out loud even Duffy cuts his lumber exactly right on the very first attempt. The Kid starts to wonder about himself, but, by golly, he finally stares proudly at three pieces of oak that are of equal length. Well, almost equal.

The Kid screws the legs to the shelves, and stands back to review his masterpiece. The end table stands fairly straight, and The Kid figures if you lean just a whisper the sucker gets a couple degrees straighter. It takes a few pounds of wood filler to fill up the gaps between the legs and the shelves, but, what the hey, Rome wasn't built in a day. The whizzers gather around and tell The Kid what a grand job he's done, but when they shuffle away The Kid hears the snickers, making him reassess his job of work. Still looks okay to The Kid. Doesn't even wobble too much.

A few days later The Kid is standing at the far corner of the playground with Davey and Duffy and a few lost souls who don't count too much observing the big boys shooting mibs. The Kid fingers his empty marble bag, lamenting the fact that he never got the hang of shooting mibs, never would. His mind is focusing in on ways to replace his stock, but his borrowing days in the old homestead has run out. Even Sis's purse has a lock on it.

Davey nudges him in the ribs, motions to shooter who the wisenheimers call Dog, but not to his face, in a game of mibs with Hooter. We're gonna get that bastard."

"You must be nuts," says The Kid.

"You weren't there when," Davey says with a superior air, "Dog pounded the hell outa Richie."

The Kid may not have seen it, but he's heard all about it. Richie is this loner who trails behind the gang nutsin' along to school. Richie ain't much for talking, kinda meek and mild and a bit slow where books are concerned. Anyway, Dog has this reputation of a buster who goes out of his way to pound the pee out of any whizzer he's got by size and weight. He nails Richie one day after school and, as advertised, pounds the pee outa Richie for no reason at all.

"Watch Richie's shoes."

Richie's clodhoppers ain't that high on The Kid's noticing list. "So?"

"Got holes in his shoes."

"So?"

"Jeez, yer thick."

The Kid takes a gander at Hooter and Dog shooting marbles, sees Richie drag his holey boots across the circle. Richie looks scared, but a few minutes later he makes another pass, slow, very deliberate. Cripes, thinks The Kid, even that dunce Dog can't miss what's happening. Suddenly, Dog jumps up and tosses Richie to the ground. "Thief, he yells. Richie is doing some first class yelling too, and the rest of the East End wisenheimers join in, cussing up a storm, pushing and shoving.

Around the corner comes the Graves, eyes lit up, trained on the confusion. He grabs Richie and Dog by their necks.

"What in the of. ." He catches himself, "is going on now?"

"He stole my marbles," charges Dog.

"Did not," returns Richie sniffling.

"Did too."

"Did not."

"Got 'em in his shoes," shouts Dog.

Mr. Graves runs his fingers through Richie's soles, proclaims them to be marble free. Pointing to the surrounding horde he asks, "Did anybody see Richie steal any marbles?"

Heads nod from side to side. Murmuring nahs come from the East End solidarity group.

"Nobody saw a thing?" The Graves has a thin smile twitching about his lips.

Silence.

"That settles it. No more marbles for the rest of the semester. And," running his orbs over the assembled misfits," all of you are confined to your homerooms until further notice."

"You mean all DAY?" This from the instigator, Davey Jackson.

With a big time glare that extends full circle to one and all, Mr. Graves marches Dog off to the principal's office.

The Kid sidles up to Davey, says in all seriousness. "You put Richie up to this? Dog'll kill him."

"Got that right, Bobby. Like you say, damn fine plan."

"Dog may be dumb, but sooner or later he'll figure he's been had."

"So?"

"He'll pound the tar out of Richie. And," The Kid notes with a grin, "what happens when Richie rats out to Dog that you put him up to it."

"Got that covered," smirks Davey. "Richie promised to tell Dog that it was you who planned his revenge."

"Me!" Shouts The Kid.

"Not to worry. The word's out yer taking boxing lessons from Kid Dempsey, who as one and all know won the title in Chicago. Dog ain't gonna pick on you."

"But," The Kid sputters, "what if he does?"

"Maybe oughta talk it over with yer brother, Bud."

"WHAT! YOU MEAN I HAVE TO KEEP THEM IN DURING RECESS?"

Miss Buler rarely raised her voice, but facing Mr. Graves the red line on her thermometer shot to the top. As the shop teacher took off for safer ground she honed in on the rascals who were responsible for her loss of freedom. Recess, it appeared, meant as much, maybe more, to her as the whizzers.

Hostility washed through McKinley's walls, and discipline became the order of classroom life. Even medium sized snickers produced hysterical responses. It seemed questionable to The Kid whether any of the East End's best and brightest would ever reach adulthood.

Two by two they went to the blackboard. Fifty times they wrote: "I will not swear. I will not fight," chalky promises that, with the wipe of an eraser, vanished from board and mind alike.

Removing chalk from the blackboards wasn't too difficult a task, but pounding the erasers together to remove the powder would about affixiate the normal breathing system. After identifying the culprit of the day, Miss Buler would escort the wise guy up to the roof to perform the lung-infecting job. Smacking the chalk dust out of those erasers became a way of life, and for the harassed teacher, a superior form of punishment.

Voice up an octave, her yardstick pointing at the cringing bodies, Miss Buler leaped at the victim of the day. "I'VE HAD IT WITH YOU. UP TO THE ROOF, and I don't want to see a SPECK OF DUST left on those erasers." A gleam of retribution flashed from her eyes as she ranted on about the worthless hide of the malcontent who had the odious task of cleaning her precious erasers. As she led her victim to the roof, her final shot was predictable, eternal and everlasting:

"DO YOU HEAR ME?"

Lord Almighty, the whole East End could hear her.

In spite of her threats to do bodily harm, pounding erasers wasn't such a bad deal. Once on the roof the Mississippi and the railroad tracks were in full view. Filled with coal or machinery, barges coasted up and down the river and freight trains whistled their way across country headed for where ever. The Kid could see all the way downtown from McKinley's roof, farther than Grennel's steeple where Davey nearly peed himself straight to jail.

While The Kid is spending his recess time clouding up the sky with chalk dust he could hear the girls in the playground laughing away as free as all get out. But it didn't bother him a whit. If this is punishment, he'd take 'er every day.

Davey Jackson spent more time on the roof than The Kid or anybody else. Davey must have been destined to be a steeplejack or some high wire artist because he sure gravitated to heights. A pure sharpie, Davey figured out that if his rights to recess were being denied by an insensitive school system, he would simply outfox authority by gaining access to the roof as often as possible.

Davey may not have been much for that book learning stuff, but when it came to planning mischief he was the at the head of the class. Miss Buler never figured out that her punishment was, in fact, a prize, but then again some teachers had more concrete upstairs than the beauts they taught.

During recess Mary Lou spots Davey on the roof so often

she directs a chorus of badmouthing at the sucker that so riles him up he complains to The Kid. Says ML calls him simple minded with a dirty mouth that offends Davey because he says he only swears when he has cause. Which is most of the time.

But The Kid doesn't have any answers for Davey. As long as Mary Lou has somebody else as a target, The Kid says fine and dandy. Anyway, what happens next is ML's fault. So sayeth The Kid.

Davey is steamed up one day something fierce, claims that ML is blabbing to her mother about his horrible conduct in school, about how Davey is always on the roof filling the landscape with eraser dust because he is simply a nasty boy. This story, of course, goes from ML's Ma directly to Davey's Ma, which is the last straw. Bringing his parents into the scene is, according to the desperate East Ender, the act of a totally corrupt person.

This confrontation, well, yelling if you want the truth of the matter, goes on and on and on. ML jeers at Davey for being the class dummy, and with all her toadies backing her up she shouts loud enough for everyone to hear how Davey's mother is at her wits end wondering what she is going to do with her wayward son. The Kid knows these girl-type taunts can't go on forever without Davey blowing up.

So one fine fall day the shop teacher is waltzing around the playground with a lively prance to his step when the first explosion happens. KERWHAP. A paper bag filled with water just misses ML by a whisker. In quick succession more water bags hit the playground. KERWHAP. KERWHAP. KERWHAP. The girls' scatter, but Mary Lou, the slowest human on two feet, does get a teensy bit wet. Ha! She is darned near drowned. The Graves snaps out of his revere and heads for the roof.

When the Gunga Din of McKinley grade school spots the shop teacher in high gear, he toots retreat and races down the stairs. With all the screaming and hollering on the playground

Miss Buler has a sudden burst of intuition. Davey Jackson, she shouts, and dashes for the roof.

At the door to the roof, Davey, Miss Buler, and Mr. Graves meet. Well, meet is hardly the word. The homeroom teacher gets knocked off her feet and while the shop teacher wastes valuable time picking her up Davey gives them the old limp leg and heads down the hall. The old Graves isn't any slouch at running, and finally he catches Davey. With an arm lock around the poor bugger's neck, he drags Davey directly to the principal's office.

Meanwhile pandemonium reigns on the playground; teachers fly around comforting a hysterical group of girls who are frozen stiff staring at a soppy Mary Lou. Without any direct supervision the East Enders are waving their fists out the window as if the revolution has just started. McKinley is up for grabs.

Of course the authorities that be take a dim view of Davey Jackson's conduct. He is expelled for a week during which time he receives a verbal battering from his mother and a physical pounding from his old man.

The Kid talks to Davey through the Jackson's screen door that is as close as Davey's mother will allow him. Davey says the whole event is blown way out of reason, and to tell the guys he'll be back. Davey swears The Kid to secrecy, says that his parents are not all that sore at him because they're fed up with Mary Lou's mother who is all the time putting on superior airs and cautioning them about their no good son. When Mrs. Johnson blabs to the neighbors that Davey ought to be put straight away in a reformatory, Davey's father threatens to beat the tar out of Mr. Johnson. But Mary Lou's Dad is only this side of a ninety pound weakling so Davey's Pa just sits on the front porch glaring across at Mary Lou's house. Davey gets a kick out of all this. Says the Johnson house is mighty quiet these days.

There must have been a big teacher's meeting because the recesses were restored. Except, of course, for Davey who sits in the principal's office with his eyes on the window. The Kid never worries about Davey -- one look into those twinkling blues and he knows Davey's mind was a clicking. Another day, another scheme. They couldn't keep his pal Davey penned up forever. But The Kid feels kinda sorry for Mr. Graves. Shoot fire, The Kid can't figure out why the Graves was in such a sour mood.

The teachers at McKinley did their best to uplift the vision of their charges. Creating a cultural atmosphere was an iffy proposition at best, but every so often special programs were presented in the auditorium, painters, dancers, and gymnasts did their best to impress the little people. Insensitive to the arts, the performances were lost on The Kid and his merry band of no-nothings. If you didn't hit it with a bat or shoot it through a hoop their minds went blank.

But they cheered the artistry of ping-pong players and did back flips over the Asian experts who performed their special Yo-Yo magic –- round the world, walking the dog and baby in the cradle. All the busters spent their stash for a brand new Duncan Yo-Yo, and for weeks tried to duplicate the wizardry seen in McKinley's auditorium. Not even *Tom Mix and His Ralston Straight Shooters* or *Captain Midnight* interfered with The Kid's after school Yo-Yo practice. Waste of time according to Ma. Ma's logic, thinks The Kid, needs to be refined.

Anyway, Miss Gorman who has a thing about teaching music announces that the music man from downtown will be putting on a show, and for heaven's sake pay attention and BE QUIET. Being new to the teaching game Miss Gorman isn't any attention getter but every once in a while her voice assumes that quarrelsome tone. Even the busters know when to pack it in.

The Kid is quietly listening to the music man blow the trumpet and trombone and is mighty impressed. During his performance the music man declares for only fifty cents a week and no down payment the busters can own an instrument and get lessons to boot. He toots some more and assembly cheers every high note. The guy is good, darned good.

Then he points to a few squirts, inviting them up to the stage to try out an instrument. Being one of the select few, The Kid tromps up and grabs a trumpet in his sweaty paw. Feeling like the school's all-time idiot, he blows a pitiful note to which the music man declares The Kid has a natural talent for the horn.

Encouraged by the cheers, The Kid blows a few more choice notes that, if the truth be said, sound like a blowout on Pete Benson's Model A. The music man presses a trumpet into The Kid's mitts and orders him to take 'er home. "The Mrs. will be right proud of you."

Ma is ecstatic. Shelling out one of the big silver coins every week isn't exactly one of Ma's strong suits, but if the music man believes he's got it she's willing to pay the price. Except for Sis who plunks away at the piano that is a couple of centuries old, making with ah-ah-AH-ah-ahs up and down the scale, there isn't much musical talent floating around the bungalow. Ma envisions Sis as the lead soprano in the church choir, and now with The Kid blowing the bricks out of the homestead Ma beams with pride. The neighbors smile and hope Ma is on the money, but in the privacy of their own homes they have their doubts. Sis is okay, but their judgement on The Kid is on hold. Wait and see is their motto.

But The Kid is a fooler. After a few weeks he has his debut on McKinley's stage. Even his pals clap when he belts out *Old Black Joe*. The upshot is that Lenny Tremains and Ralphie Jones sign up for trumpets. The music man has it in mind to unload a few clarinets and saxophones, but the busters figure if the trumpet is good enough for The Kid it is good enough for them. All told, six trumpets disappear into the whizzer's mitts and the East End brass section is born.

In order to preserve his sanity and collect a few bucks the music man arranges a once a week collective lesson at one of the tooter's homes. It's loud. It is pathetic. Prunes and Red do a disappearing act every time the trumpeters show up. The sessions even test Ma's ability to smile, but she holds her head high while the notes blast her eardrums.

Problem for The Kid is that the music man chews. Course he spits out his Red Man chaw before the lesson starts, but every time he uses The Kid's instrument to teach some fine point of trumpet artistry The Kid gags on the stained mouthpiece when it is his turn to play. Ralphie Jones says that chewing is a right manly thing to do, kinda likes the taste. The Kid figures that if he bottles the music man's saliva he can make a fortune in the shellac business.

The off-key blaring from a bunch of rope-necked, blow-cheeked whizzers disrupted the neighborhood's peace and quiet –- Dads and Grandpas were to be found down at the Belgium Village hoisting a brew or ten –- but the proud mothers heard a different beat. Being a whole lot closer to the scene of the crime, The Kid decides that mothers would go to any lengths deceiving themselves.

So the band played on.

As fall turned into winter, The Kid becomes more accustomed to the big house they called McKinley. Between teacher and student a truce of sorts had been called. Dismal looking midterm report cards had brought forth the howls of righteous parents who threatened their offspring. In the hands of a disturbed parent, the leather strap was the usual instrument of terror. Since Christmas was not far away, the possibility of ashes instead of presents pressured the wisenheimers to pick up their books. Teachers were happy, classrooms had quieted down, learning was on the rise, and parents were seen to smile.

The end table, a bit shaky perhaps and maybe not quite plumb, worried The Kid. Mr. Graves deadline was fast approaching. The project had to be completed by Christmas break, and The Kid was dead last. The stain was okay, but somehow The Kid messed up the varnish. The end table simply would not dry.

Each day, expecting to get that nice smooth feeling he'd run his fingers gingerly over the surface. And each day the stickiness remained.

The Kid's mighty depressed and his attitude is getting to be a drag on his buddies. He sits in shop with a sad-punk face swearing under his breath *ordering* that danged table to dry out. Mr. Graves passes him by without a word. Davey and the Hooter and H who are already dreaming up projects for the next semester shake their heads and mumble words of encouragement, but the old end table sits there, a sticky mess that refuses to dry.

One day Hooter suggests that The Kid put the disaster in the furnace room. Needs a little heat says the H. Hmmm, thinks The Kid, not a bad idea. When the janitor spies The Kid's dream table he asks all sarcastic-like if The Kid wants him to throw it in the furnace with the rest of the trash.

"Make right nice kindling," he roars. "Maybe put 'er out of its misery," he roars some more.

The Kid takes the umbrage in style. Says, "If you don't mind, sir, if we give it a few days next to the furnace, it'll be just dandy."

The janitor shoots The Kid a shifty glance, "And I guess you expect Santa Claus to climb down your chimney, too."

On the last day before Christmas break The Kid takes a final walk to the furnace room. Mr. Graves and his buddies watch him shuffle down the corridor knowing full well that his project will forever be a gluey mess. The Kid pauses at the furnace room door, hesitates, pulls his shoulders up like Ma says he's supposed to do. And discovers a truth which he carries with him forever:

The Good Lord looks out for fools and little busters without a lick of talent.

The janitor beams, says, "Sonny, you are the luckiest kid alive. I was about to pitch that danged joke in the furnace, just to save you the embarrassment, mind you, when, lo and behold, the critter don't stick to my hands."

The Kid passes his hand across the tabletop and it is slicker'n beeswax. Recovery from certain disaster is, he decides, a wonderful happening. The Kid puffs up a bit, and the janitor opens the door and gives him a pat on the back.

When he walks in carrying his end table, Mr. Graves puts his arm around The Kid's shoulders and tells him what a fine job he has done. His buddies stand around telling him how they always believed in his woodworking ability and a bunch of other lies, and The Kid makes a sweeping bow and says thank you very much.

When The Kid gives Ma the end table for Christmas she smiles the most wonderful smile The Kid had ever seen. Plunks it down right in the living room, says it's there for keeps. Prunes allows as to how he couldn't have done better which is a bit much, but it is Christmas and all.

The Kid knows his project ain't any great shakes, but, gosh darn it, it gets better looking every time he swipes it a glance. Leans a little to port, but if Ma likes it that is all that counts.

When Ma's happy The Kid's happy.

BOYS IF I COULD DO IT, I'D DO IT MYSELF

Bud, Ma, Bob, Cully Johnson

Being the eldest son, Prunes took The Kid's practical education to heart, teaching him by example. When The Kid didn't understand the goings-on in the adult world, Prunes would set him straight. It wasn't just that Prunes was so much older, but it was the way Prunes gave advice that impressed The Kid. He was serious and studious and had umpteen ideas about how to do this or that. Give him a problem and Prunes figured out the answer. Prunes never circled the wagons, never nutsed around just to make The Kid feel better. Told him straight out. The Kid admired Prunes.

Prunes was a true genius with his hands that had nothing to do with earlier years that had him kicking the beegeebers out of some East End tough who was dumb enough to besmirch the family name. Which, by the way, happened often enough because Prunes could spot a slur from about a zillion miles away. No sir, Prunes' genius lay in woodworking, fixing anything that needed fixing, putting his education to practical uses - most of the time.

He was forever getting these bursts of inspiration that he translated into some important project. The old idea bulb would flash in his noggin and he'd go to the library and study up a storm, then pester the men who worked in the shops about the best way to do this or that. When Prunes was possessed, look out.

This old water heater had been lying in the basement for a couple a centuries or so, and Prunes saw in that thick steel cylinder the makings of a diving helmet that, if he did it right, could be used by the U.S. Navy. It took him a week to file off the top, which if you think about it tells you something about how tenacious Prunes was. Then he hacked out two curved sections so that it would fit around his shoulders, chest and back. When he was walking around the briny deep Prunes decided he had to see what was going on fish-wise, so he cut out a rectangle right there where his eyes would be. Since he only had a file it took him forever. Prunes was fairly struck with Ma's determination. By golly, if it could be done, he'd do it.

He cornered this old geezer Frank Nelson who lived in a shack down the alley, to help him make a faceplate with a piece of glass in it. Frank worked in a foundry and possessed the tangy odor of sweat and iron. The Kid used to watch Frank as he walked up the alley to the woods with a piece of newspaper in his hand to do his daily duty. According to Prunes the old scutter is a pretty smart guy and helpful as all get out. Prunes' nostrils probably did a dodge when he was deep in conversation with the aromatic foundry man, but what was a stinky smell when Prunes was after the secrets of underwater science? Prunes was so caught up with the idea that he'd be able see all the important things there was to see when he was in the briny deep. He dreamed of fish and squishy critters and marine life in all its purest. When he wasn't filing away like a madman, he had his head in a book making notes about what's happening on the riverbed.

He bolts the faceplate around the hole he had cut out and drills a hole in the top for the air hose connection. He stands back with a satisfied grin on his puss. All in all this is a superior diving helmet, one decorated with a blue ribbon.

Prunes calls on Frank once again, asks how in the world will he be able to stand on the bottom without tipping over. Next day Frank appropriates two heavy iron bars from the foundry, and Prunes using a couple of leather belts drapes the iron bars over his shoulders. Then with great difficulty (the water heater must have weighed a ton) Prunes fits the helmet over his head. It is tight as can be. The Kid watches open-mouthed, amazed with his brother's ingenuity, proud just to know him.

Prunes decides that he'll have Red and Swede in the row boat pumping away on an old bicycle pump, delivering the atmosphere to him through a rubber tube. This isn't the greatest answer to Prunes requirement for air, but he believes fully in Ma's saying that necessity was the mother of invention. In this case, necessity was a bicycle pump and two unreliable agents, Red and Swede.

The Kid takes in Prunes enthusiastic blathering, but is surprised at his older brother's naive trust in his fellow conspirators -- Red and Swede to be precise. The Kid wouldn't have trusted Red and Swede to walk him to the edge of the river, let alone put his life in their hands. But with the certainty of a cause that blinds a leader to personal danger, Prunes dismisses

The Kid's premonition of danger. The Mississippi today, the Atlantic tomorrow is his motto.

Berserk with his objective he makes the final touches, files a bit here and there, stands back to admire his work, grins and frowns as the mood hits him. Figures that some admiral will call him any day now:

"Navy needs your diving bell, Prunes." And Prunes replies, "Yes sir, glad to help the navy, Sir."

It bothers The Kid no end when Prunes talks to himself with his eyes glazed over, but he decides that Prunes was onto something really big. Red, of course, wasn't about to waste his time watching Prunes sweat bullets while talking to somebody that wasn't there so he bugs out. As Ma was fond of saying, Red had other fish to fry.

The sole obstacle that diverts Prunes' attention to his project was Ma. She had projects of her own for The Boys: mowing the lawn, weeding the garden, cleaning the screens, painting the storm windows, or spending a day sacking potatoes at Baker's Dairy farm to pay for the milk bill. Ma parceled out these chores with the firmness of a Marine Top Sarge ordering the troops to shape up.

Each summer Ma had a load of wood delivered. Huge blocks of hard wood which Ma paid next to nothing for and which were used, along with the coal, to heat the bungalow in the winter. A big truck would back up on one side of the house and dump the load. The Boys would proceed to heave the blocks through the basement window. The windows were small so they had to be careful not to hit the frame.

Ma informs Prunes and Red that the delivery is coming today and for them to be close by so that they can toss the wood into the basement and to be careful this year as she is sick and tired of seeing the window frame all busted up, and WERE THEY LISTENING?

In unison, The Boys gave her a disgusted reply to which she said: "Boys, if I could do it, I'd do it myself."

Resigned to his fate, Prunes knows he has to work on that darned pile of wood. Shoot, if he doesn't get in a trial run with his diving bell pretty soon some highbinder'll come along and steal his idea and get all those government contracts he envisions coming his way. So when he raises the basement window, he's ready to work.

Red stands there, assessing the situation. Well, that's a bit of a reach. Red is really dogging it. He knows full well that Prunes is as antsy as Blackie Cole's dog and if Red don't interfere too much Prunes'll do all the work. The Kid figures Red is the cleverest guy alive.

Meanwhile, Ma's in the basement supervising the project. Not too long into the pile old Prunes is a steaming along, throwing those blocks of wood in the window like a crazed man. Ma's yelling at him to slow down because if he doesn't watch what he's doing he'll hit the window frame, and all she needed was to have these dimwits busting up the house. As certain as lightning follows thunder, Prunes takes out the whole window frame with a big chunk of wood, and there was, speaking mildly, hell to pay. Ma's screaming at him to stop, but Prunes pumps the wood in faster than ever. Swears later that he didn't hear her.

Red, the designated number two hitter, mentions to Prunes that he ought to slow down otherwise they were going to have to build an entire new side to the house. But Prunes keeps throwing in the blocks. All he can think of is the wasted time away from his pet diving bell project. And Red ain't helping any -- great supervisor, but slow on the uptake when it comes to exertion.

Ma's mighty disgusted. Prunes wasn't paying any attention to her, so she steps closer to the window to give him a good old fashioned what for and one of Prunes' throws catches her square on the foot. Holy smokers, did she yelp, and moan, and mutter. And yelp, and moan, and mutter.

Like a fox fleeing the hounds, Red disappears at top speed. Brother, he was gone. Prunes who by this time is coming out of his trance, finally realizes that he had decked Ma with a high hard one. The Kid sees Prunes' ashen face and wonders just how fast he can run.

Prunes is scared, no doubt about it, but he screws up his courage and trots on down to the basement where Ma is holding her foot and moaning something fierce. Between the moans Ma mutters about those ungrateful whelps that just wouldn't listen and, by golly, if she could do it she'd do it herself. Prunes was all conciliatory, sweet as all get out, but Ma wasn't responding.

Silence. Finally, Prunes goes back to the woodpile, and with The Kid helping out, he finishes the chore.

Prunes makes a new window frame that, in all honesty, was better than the original. And he stacks the wood nice and neat-like the way Ma wanted it done. Ma limps around the house for a few days and gives Prunes the silent treatment that in her house was prime time punishment because Ma weren't the silent type.

The most Red gets is a few grunts which means that Ma's really mad because Red could always wheedle a smile out of her. Prunes thinks about Red running off and the more he thinks about it the madder he gets. He wants to bring Red's desertion under fire to Ma's attention, but decides he'd better keep his mouth shut because Ma's so mad at him that she'll probably add the charge of squealing onto his record which by this time was mighty black indeed.

The Kid never remembered Ma ever supervising the wood detail again. Bitter memories probably. Anyway, the project was finished and the diving helmet looked really neat. Prunes had given the old water heater-diving helmet a coat of tan paint. The rivets were done in black. Standing with those stupid weights hung on his chest and the helmet over his head, he looked like some skinny Martian with bug eyes and a voice that came out of a tunnel. The Kid expected him to say, "Take me to your leader," but decided this was no time for frivolity.

Red and Swede allowed as to how they considered their role

in this epic venture real heart warming and claimed Prunes didn't have a worry in the world with them standing ready at the pump. Prunes issued final instructions to the two delinquents, and they headed for the river pulling the diving helmet and weights in The Kid's wagon. Destiny beckoned.

Although the Cubs were thrashing the Boston Braves again The Kid snapped off the broadcast and tagged along. Just being an eyewitness to history in the making might increase his standing with his own buddies.

Down at the river Mr. Erickson waited expectantly for Prunes. Pointing to his rowboat he says, "take 'er out." Which is mighty kindly for old Erickson. The Kid sidles up to the smoked fish man like an old hound dog waiting patiently for a morsel, and when the fisherman sits down to watch The Kid follows suit. Figures he'll get a piece of that smoked fish before the day is over.

The three aquanauts pile in the rowboat. The bozos almost drop the diving bell in the water, and the boat lists dangerously to one side, but off they go rowing slowly to deep water.

The Kid wonders if success will spoil Prunes, and hopes it won't go to his head when the president or some admiral calls him to offer congratulations. Watching his hero strapping on the weights The Kid remembers Prunes telling him that they must be on good and tight to give him proper balance, that if he didn't have balance he might tip over and ruin the dive. Then Red and Swede pop the helmet over his shoulders, and with a wave of his hand Prunes goes over the side and into the Mississippi. Convinced that history was in the making, The Kid has a lump in his throat. Here he sat, related by blood to the famous diver.

What transpired in the next few minutes was more than a bit confusing. Red and Swede are jawing away at each other. Red pumps a few times, and then he and Swede argue about whether Prunes had enough air. The wisenheimers didn't want to overdo it, didn't want Prunes too full up with oxygen. Meanwhile Prunes goes straight down, at an alarming rate, in fact. When he hits bottom his feet sink deep in the muddy bottom, and to his dismay he can't move. Not up, not sideways, not noways. To complicate his peril Prunes miscalculated on the amount of air that would be required -- miscalculated disastrously. The pump could hardly fill a miserable bicycle tire let alone get the air twenty feet down to his helmet. Prunes recognizes immediately that he is in deep, no pun intended, trouble. He pulls on the rubber tube, but realizes that the pumpers who hold his life in their miserable hands, aren't pumping.

Worried he should have been because at this moment Red and Swede are assessing their chances of expropriating some keen item from one of the locals who don't know Monday from Tuesday. Laughing at the possibility of an easy mark, their enthusiasm for the bicycle pump had dimmed. Stopped pumping, is what they did.

About this time Prunes is turning blue, and in desperation he bends forward and fights the diving helmet off his head. In near panic he unties the straps that hold the weights and he shoots to the surface like a dolphin arcing out of the ocean. Lordy, when he appears all sudden-like, Red leaps to the pump, knowing in an instant that he was about to be blamed for whatever had happened on the river bottom. But Prunes ain't about to talk, just splashes around all ashen and blue, gasping for breath. Swede and Red grab him and tug him into the boat. Prunes lay in the gunnels, gesturing and moaning about his brush with certain death.

"Why the hell weren't you pumping?"

Red stammers, "We didn't see any air bubbles."

"YOU DIDN'T SEE ANY BUBBLES!"

The Kid sure don't know what had happened, but he knows his chance for reflected glory had been lost in the Mississippi mud. There wouldn't be any calls from the White House now. He considers asking Prunes a couple scientific questions, but listening to the poor sucker moaning he keeps his trap shut. This wasn't the time to aggravate a man in pain.

When color comes back to Prunes' face, he starts yelling about the bends and what a fool he was putting his life in Red's hands, and what in the name of hell had they been doing, for Pete's sake. Red and Swede stand there tap dancing around Prunes' accusations, silently taking it all in. The Kid scampers home.

Somehow Prunes recovers the diving helmet, but the weights were lost forever. Pulling their slightly used cargo home the threesome deliver the diving helmet to a permanent home in a corner of the basement, never to be used again. Sort of like the Spruce Goose -- one voyage, then consigned to history.

It takes Prunes a while to admit that something serious had flawed his experiment, but in the back of his mind the thought persists that a better effort by Red and Swede might have spelled the difference between victory and defeat. The Kid never forgets Prunes popping out of the water like a stricken shark, ashen and pale and blue, and he laments the fact that the Navy wasn't going to call after all.

But old Prunes is one tough guy. His disappointment probably lasted for a day. Maybe. He wasn't the type to cry over missed chances at fame. Onward and upward was Prunes' motto. One day when he's nutsin' along up around Swallows Cliff he spots an old wagon standing in Fred Hines's barnyard. With weeds covering its wheels, the wagon had obviously been put to pasture. So with the diving helmet tucked away in the basement and his aquanaut's adventure a thing of the past, Prunes turns his attention to the farm wagon.

He surveys the farm for days on end to make certain the wagon was history. Well, the more degenerate members of the East End crew consider appropriating the wagon without permission even though none of the misfits know exactly why they wanted the darn thing. Shoot, even Prunes, he of the wise decisions, isn't too sure why he wanted the wagon or what he'd do once he got his mitts on it. But one thing he was sure of. He was going to have THAT WAGON.

Which prompted the East End band of merry men to get into the surveillance business. By day and night that old piece of junk received more attention than it had ever had in its entire working life. Finally one of the roustabouts says to Prunes why don't he just walk on over to Fred Hines and ask him for the damn thing.

After some heavy thought Prunes screws up his courage and does just that. He steps up to farmer Hines with that proud Prunes look and admits he'd sure like to have that sucker. Prunes gets all apologetic-like telling the farmer how he'd take good care of his prized possession and that his wagon would be going to a good cause, and blah, blah, blah. When Prunes starts rambling there's no stopping him, probably stayed up all night practicing his speech.

The farmer looks at Prunes as if the lad has lost his marbles. Fred Hines had wondered for the longest time when the Good Lord was going to send him some poor sap to remove the worthless, decrepit wagon off his property, and here stands the answer to his prayers. "If that's what you want son, just go ahead and take 'er." The farmer smiles, slaps Prunes on the back and wishes him well.

Well sir, when Prunes took aholt of the wagon tongue he just about drove himself into the ground trying to move the blamed critter. Then he gives it a closer gander. The wagon is a flat bed high-riser, all wood construction with wood-spoke wheels about four feet in diameter, a big sucker no matter which way you eyed it. It doesn't look particularly heavy, but it takes the whole crew of misfits, including Red and Swede, to haul it home.

Ma takes one peep at the monstrosity and asks whose fool idea it was to cart that piece of junk into her back yard. So Prunes has another selling job to do. Stands up right tall and all and tells Ma that this piece of junk might be the wave of the future. Says that modern-day transportation deserves his undivided attention and if she will give him a smidgen of time to figure out the best way to put this marvelous device into use she sure won't be sorry. Why, maybe the president or one of his cabinet members is waiting right this minute for a brand new discovery on how to move the population cheaper and faster.

Ma gives Prunes the fish eye, allows as to how *her* basement was filling up with new and better inventions to do this or that, and that no one to her knowledge, especially the president, had called, and was that water heater-diving helmet going to rest forever in *her* basement? The Neanderthals stand there with the usual blank stares on their maps listening to the exchange, hoping Ma doesn't address any questions to them as none of the light weights know what in Hades they are doing, or why. The conspirators have a vague impression, fostered by Prunes of course, that all they have to do is give the creaky wagon a little fixin' up and then they'll all have the time of their lives. These guys smile a lot, probably due to the wind whistling through their ears.

Ma's waiting for Prunes to say something brilliant, and Prunes is wishing Red would speak up and save the day. But Red registers the thought that if Ma is really upset about the wagon there ain't any reason for him to take the heat off Prunes. The red head shuffles his shoes and peers down the alley, and a general silence confronts Ma. Staring at the assembled faces, Ma shakes her head and trots back to the kitchen. Prunes takes her exit for an okay, but wishes Ma had a little more faith in his ideas. He turns to the malcontents and says, "Let's get at it, time's a wasting."

Off come the wheels, the spokes are cinched up and the metal rims repaired. The axles are cleaned and greased, and the wagon tongue, a wobbly old stick, made fast. Prunes makes a brand-new wagon bed and a coat of red lead is applied to it. After several days of working in the hot sun, the Neanderthals view their project with pride -- the sucker takes on the grandeur of days long past. Prunes' enthusiasm and vigor grows day by day. The guy is plain project oriented. The dismal experience of the ill-fated diving helmet was an event lost in time.

The Kid figures Prunes simply has a short memory. Heard of people like that, kinda idiot-like, forgetful as all get out. He wonders if Prunes hadn't been under the old Missisip too long without air because he had heard that the lack of oxygen destroys the brain cells and if that was the case the only cards Prunes held were the jokers. Least ways, that's what Russ down at the gas station contended.

But, brother, could Prunes work. Ma probably looked at him with every intention of channeling all that energy into something positive or, at the very least, something more useful to her. Red watched him, too, but careful-like so as to not catch the fever.

Right in the middle of the project yellow jaundice knocks Prunes and Red mighty low. This old bones of a doctor tells Ma that day-old rye bread and beer have a mysterious therapeutic effect on jaundice patients, and he prescribes a bottle of beer a day for The Boys. Claims it will give them their strength back. Ma inquires if the brew will bring back a natural color to The Boys faces, being by now a pale yellow, and the doc says sure enough. Just shove the rye down their gullets and let them guzzle a few beers every day and they will be right as rain.

Wondering where Ma finds these beauts that call themselves medical men, The Kid listens to the bone cutter expound on the value of malt and hops. The Boys nod their heads in a way that says if they are forced to drink beer they will, but only in the advance of medical science, mind you. Had they been feeling better Ma would have belted them.

Ma takes charge ordering in the malt and hops and whatever it takes to brew beer. While The Boys and The Kid watch from the basement steps she throws the magic ingredients into a huge kettle, and talks a lot about the proper period of fermentation as if she had been in the business all her life.

The Kid thinks there's nothing that Ma can't do. Some of

the neighbors haul in bushel baskets of inky-brown beer bottles which Ma steps around as agile as a ballerina as she goes about her task. The basement is filled with kettles of brew fermenting, baskets of newly washed bottles, and cans of hops and malt. Ma races downtown to buy a bottle capper, and when she gets the hang of it, she starts filling the bottles and capping them at a near record rate.

That night the explosions begin. Bottle caps banging against the basement ceiling are making Ma darned disgusted. Complains about the cheap equipment the merchants are passing off on naive customers these days. Ma inspects the A-1 Bottle capper for flaws, mutters a lot, but gets better at the capping process and is soon producing beer that stays put in the bottle. The Boys require beer and Ma sees to it they have what the sawbones prescribed.

Each night Ma serves Prunes and Red a bottle of home brew. And she likes her draught, too. Suddenly there are pretzels on the kitchen table making it an evening event. During the day Prunes woebegone puss stares at the wagon taking up half the backyard. He and Red are too fatigued to argue, just lazing around the house yellow faced and all.

But in the evening, they perk up a bit and swallow the home brew gratefully. No more talk of being guinea pigs serving the interests of science. Ma holds forth producing her pearls of wisdom and The Boys nod with apparent interest. When Ma pours a small glass for The Kid, Sis lets it be known she doesn't think this is a wise idea, The Kid being a minor and all that. But Ma says it was okay, and The Kid sips away and stuffs down pretzels and considers the occasion a wonderful time.

The Kid shoulda known better, but being a little squirt he ain't too long on deep thought. During the day he brags to his buddies about how Ma allows him to swill up a glass of suds just like his brothers and what a treat it is. His buddies look at The Kid with renewed respect. Among the shavers, The Kid is a big man. Fact is he was the only one of his traveling companions that was permitted to drink just like grown-ups.

So one of the squealers tells his parents that The Kid's coughing up the suds every night, and that Ma is forcing her sons to drink the evil brew against their collective wills. The lie spreads throughout the East End and one of Ma's lady friends informs her most sweetly that the wind was up, temperance wise. Well sir, that night when Ma serves the brew, The Kid sits there on empty eating pretzels, getting dryer by the minute. Ma ignores his wimpy cough and talks to The Boys about how much better they seemed to be. The Kid gets the idea that things ain't going too well, but is smart enough not to ask why.

"Well," Ma says pointing a pretzel at The Kid, "What do you have to say for yourself?"

The Kid reviews everything he had done lately, and, lo and behold believes his slate is pretty darned clean. He considers admitting that yes, he is the culprit stealing Mrs. Reece's apples, but decides against admitting anything. The Kid stammers about how clean he is, but Ma picks up on his case of the shakes, declaring for the umpteenth time that what is said in the house and what is done in the house and what happens in the house, STAYS IN THE HOUSE, and does he understand this? The Kid's shaking for good by now, figures the end has come.

Ma reports that one of the neighbors has been kind enough to inform her that The Kid's been blabbing all over the East End that he's having a gay old time swilling up beer and crunching pretzels every night, and that this story is an embarrassment to her and the family name.

The Kid is sliding down in his chair, a goner if there ever was one. There is nothing more precious to Ma than the family name. Shoot fire, even Prunes had drilled that into him from the time The Kid strapped on diapers. Finally, the big picture is coming through. Ma claims that confession is good for the soul, but The Kid ain't too sure about that.

He says that yes, he might have mentioned off-hand-like

that he was drinking a wee bit of the suds at night, but honest to goodness Ma, it was just to ward off the fever that Prunes and Red had contracted in some unknown and strange place, and that for all The Kid knows The Boys have some sort of jungle rot which they picked up in one of their mysterious adventures, or maybe had come under the spell of a Chinaman because how else can you explain their yellow faces?

Ma watches her youngest and sighs. It seems to her that the only disease he had contracted was the ability to talk around the subject without a straight out admission of guilt. She concludes that Jacky's influence on her youngest has infected his behavior badly. So Ma repeats her order: What is said in the house remains in the house. With a sad puss, The Kid nods.

And his glass remains empty, never to be filled again.

A couple of weeks later, the sawbones informs Ma that Prunes and Red are fit enough to engage in physical exertion. Red pops up and inquires if they ought not to continue sipping beer because he, for one, is of the belief it gives him strength he had never felt before. Red is good, darned good, but the bone crusher sees through him as easy as looking through a plate glass window.

Ma's sitting there fit to be tied, but smiling all the same. The doc is a pretty sharp cookie. He looks at Ma and asks her what she thinks. Ma ponders the question as if giving it all due consideration, then allows as to how in her opinion Buddy and Jacky are as close to full recovery as one could expect them to be and as far as she is concerned they don't require any beer either on or off the premises which tells The Boys she knows all about the goings on in Swede's garage.

The wagon awaits. The East End Neanderthals gather around the back yard and listen to Prunes' plans. They will pull the bugger up to the top of 48th Street hill going up the bluff, then ride it down the alley running behind Ma's house. One of the misfits asks Prunes if they could make it to the main drag and

Prunes says, nah, it'll never go that far. Besides with Red on the brake and Prunes driving, what could go wrong? All they needed was a lookout on 5th avenue to give a warning should oncoming traffic block their flight.

Prunes inspected the brake that was nothing more than a pole on a fulcrum that could be applied to one of the rear wheels, and pronounced it capable of stopping the wagon. However, he had not deemed it necessary to test its braking ability against the possible speed they were about to generate. To the crew Prunes word was law. No one questioned Prunes. Besides, if he got riled he might just pound a guy's head into the ground. But Prunes was pretty smart, too. He walked to the alley and measured the run from the top of the hill to 5th avenue. Then he turned and looked down the alley to 4th avenue, the main drag where the streetcars ran. Nah, no way would they travel that far.

The whole East End crew is pumped up. They draw lots to see who would be the first lookout on 5th avenue, and with a mighty roar and burst of energy, they pull and push the farm wagon to the top of the hill. Resting at the top, they could see all the way to the train tracks and the river.

The Kid tags along hoping, but not really expecting, that Prunes or Red would ask him aboard the maiden run. He had never seen the Neanderthals in such high spirits.

Swede pops up, says, "Hey Prunes, how about the squirt going along?"

Prunes yells, "Okay with me. Ya wanna go squirt?" The Kid runs for the wagon, and hands pull him aboard. Swede puts his arm around The Kid and the wagon begins to roll.

Slowly at first, then gaining momentum with an enormous surge the wheels roll effortlessly. When the wagon hits the bottom of the hill it is really traveling. The Kid's bouncing all over the place, his rear end banging away on the wagon bed, just a chugging along with tears running down his face from the wind. Shazam, it is great. He looks at Prunes with admiration steering the bugger unerringly down the hill, and to Red who stands up tall like George Washington himself at the tiller.

At 5th avenue Mex waves a go-ahead and the wagon speeds past him like a streak of light. About this time Prunes recognizes the possibility that they might make 4th avenue, but it wasn't until they closed in on the main drag that he signals Red to man the brake.

Well, you might just as well have tried to stop a charging elephant with a toothpick because when Red pulls at the pole, old faithful keeps right on charging. The crew begins thinking about their exit bows, but the wagon is still hammering along so fast that to jump off means a lot of busted parts. Theirs. Prayers come to the Neanderthals. The Kid knows because he sees their lips moving, talking to themselves kinda inside-like. Cheering every turn of the wheels, he is having the time of his life.

The wagon tears through 4th avenue like a berserk rhino. Mr. Thickston, one of the senior trolley car drivers who has had more than his share of the East End band of merry pranksters what with their constant disconnecting of the pole that runs up the back of the trolley to the overhead electric line, was, at the moment, almost even with the intersection of the alley and 4th avenue. Seeing imminent disaster, Mr. Thickston brakes the trolley to a screeching stop. Bodies are a bouncing all around inside the trolley, and as the wagon roars past, The Kid spies old lady Masterson fainting and clutching frantically at her pocket book all at the same time.

From the opposite direction comes Pete Benson in his almost brand new Model A Ford. Pete Benson loves his car like nothing else matters in the world, and with the sudden appearance of the wagon loaded with flying bodies, he stands upright on the brake peddle, tires screeching, groceries spilling all over the back seat. Pete comes to a stop sort of cattywumpus facing Thickston's streetcar, not breathing too well but grateful to the Lord on high who spared his Model A certain wreckage.

Somehow or another Prunes steers through the melee, and

down the alley. He shouts frantically at Red to, "pull on the damn brakes." Swede joins Red on the pole and the two suckers yank with everything they got. The Kid smells the smoke coming from the brake pole and the wagon seems to slow down. Finally it runs up the berm fronting the railroad tracks, halts, and slowly backs down.

The Neanderthals sit there glassy eyed, but The Kid cheers, knowing he just had the best darned ride a guy could ever have. His rear end was sore having hit the flatbed a zillion times during the downhill run, but shoot fire that was a small price to pay for the most daring assault run ever made in the history of the East End. Prunes looks stunned and Red, for the first time in his life, is speechless. Looking back up the alley a pile of neighbors are shaking their fists at the wagon. And its cargo.

Mr. Thickston and Pete Benson trudge toward the crew with none other than Officer Swan Larson, the local copper, in tow. Officer Larson lives down the street from Ma, a good neighbor and a friend to Ma. He works the night beat, closing all the downtown taverns when the laggards tend to get out of hand. He is a legend in his own time, and the ultimate authority figure in the East End. A cheer dies in The Kid's mouth when he spots Officer Larson bearing down on them. The main man doesn't look too happy.

He lights into The Boys something fierce about putting citizen's lives in danger, criminal damage to property, driving an unsafe vehicle on the city streets, giving heart failure to ladies in delicate condition, and placing the life of a minor, to wit, The Kid, in imminent danger of never reaching the age of ten. And what did the lummoxes say to that?

Red finds his tongue, tells the law and the assembled crowd of onlookers that they had made a slight miscalculation on the braking mechanism otherwise everything went along just dandy. He takes in Officer Larson's puss and produces a grin.

"MISCALCULATION," Officer Larson roars.

Red keeps talking, his all-American smile kinda lopsided,

but chattering away playing his trump card. Allows as to how he and Prunes are mighty weak having suffered long and hard from the dreaded yellow jaundice, and that maybe the disease had effected their brains being unable to think straight and all, and that they would never knowingly place The Kid, their little brother who they love dearly, in danger as Officer Larson knows full well that Ma would punish them from now until doomsday should anything awful happen to their beloved little brother.

Officer Larson lets Red go on, but he knows baloney when he hears it. He's as aware as anyone still kicking his heels in the East End that Red can slice it as thick or thin as the case demands. So when he listens to this yellow jaundice nonsense, he shakes his head as if to say, "Brother, I've heard them all but, Red, you're one of the best, and nothing but a snot-nosed rascal yet." He orders the crew to remove the wagon from the neighborhood within 24 hours or else the slammer awaits them.

With that, Pete Benson, a kinda sour-grapes guy, gets his two cents in, shouting to one and all that if there is so much as a scratch on his beloved Model A he's going to sue everyone involved, especially The Boys, as the whole East End knows they are the leaders of this foul bunch of malcontents that have nothing better to do but harass decent people, blah, blah, blah.

Officer Larson lets Pete run on, but it's obvious that he has enough problems without listening to the East End's Mr. Grump. He tells Pete to get his car off the main drag or else he would have to issue him a ticket, and that if there was any suing to do he'd do it, not Mr. Benson, thank you very much. Well, Pete walks away sputtering about ungrateful civil servants, but not too loudly mind you, and Mr. Thickston revs up his streetcar, and The Boys pull the wagon back to Ma's back yard.

The Kid decides that Officer Larson must have gone directly to Ma, but knows the policeman is polite and nice about it so Ma can save some face. So that night Ma is primed for them: orders the wisenheimers to get that piece of junk out of her backyard once and for all, then lays into them about putting The Kid's life in danger, and what in the name of heaven did they think they were doing? Ma's mad and embarrassed at the same time which is a no good thing if you're accustomed to peace in the old homestead.

The next day Prunes pride and joy disappears. The Kid decides Prunes probably took 'er out to some farm wagon graveyard and prayed over it. The Kid smiles to himself. That sucker sure went out in style.

With the sickly yellow tint gone from their faces, Ma once again has two able bodies to take on the chores. She's happy, back in top form. There were major tasks to be done that, optimistically, she expects them to turn to willingly. Today, this or that chore must be completed. Not tomorrow, nor next week, but TODAY. With all the moaning and excuses and crying about Ma's chores interrupting their precious schedules, you would have thought the end of the world was here and now. The Kid soaks up their excuses, each one worthless as sin, wondering why Prunes and Red take the time to argue when they were doomed. Time and again they try to get through her defenses, but fail to budge Ma an inch. Like a couple of whimpering idiots, they always cave in. Ma had them right in the palms of her hands when she laid them low with:

"Boys if I could do it, I'd do it myself."

THE OLD OAK TREE

Bob and Sis

With his toes and fingers clutched in the clay holes the swallows used as nests The Kid held tightly onto the cliff, yelling, "Watch this." Instead of doing his famous death-defying leap to safety he lost his balance and tumbled into the creek below. Listening to the jeers of his buddies The Kid's pride was mighty offended. And his clothes were soaked, too. Shoot fire, if Davey and the whizzers had wanted to play baseball none of this would have happened to him. Disgusted and embarrassed The Kid shucks his shoes and socks and trudges down the creek bed.

It was hot and humid, the kind of day that slows human adventures down to zero. Carrying his shoes and socks he sloshes down the creek bed, the minnows tickling his toes, thinking he just might wade the creek under the culverts at 5th and 4th avenues all the way down to the Mississippi. Stop by and see Mr. Erickson, maybe cadge a piece of smoked catfish. Just depend on how a guy felt. No sense jumping into big decisions without thinking them through.

At this neat pool shy of the 5th avenue culvert, one of The Kid's favorite places to do nothing at all, he hunched down and watched the water bugs skitter back and forth like a bunch of crazies. The bugs had pads for feet, and thread-like legs that zoomed them across the pool faster than anything The Kid had ever seen. Fascinated, he pondered what drove them to near frenzy, wondered if they ever went to sleep.

"What cha doing?"

Looking up The Kid spots Johnny standing on top of the culvert. "Wondering if these bugs ever get any sleep."

"Ain't ya got nothin' else to do?"

"Nope."

A good-sized boy with straw-blond hair, Johnny frowned at The Kid. "Wanna check out Chuck's penny candy?"

"Ain't got any pennies." To be sure, The Kid searched his pant's pockets. "Nope, no pennies."

"Shoot, I got a couple. Come on, I'll treat ya."

Built atop the culvert that extended under 5th avenue Chuck's grocery store was empty, customer-wise. The boys stood in front of a glass case filled with licorice and gumdrops and peppermint buttons stuck on a paper sheet, hemmed and hawed while Chuck waited patiently. The Kid could hear the creek gurgling as it ran through the culvert right under Chuck's store. One time The Kid asked Red what would happen to the store if a thunderstorm forced the creek up really, really high. Red claimed that Chuck'd probably end up in St. Louis which sounded like a long way away so, like most things he didn't want to hear, let alone think about, The Kid put that thought out of his mind.

The boys lingered in front of Chuck's store chewing on licorice sticks, one black and one red. The Kid decides it was real sporty of Johnny to treat him. Johnny was an okay guy even if The Kid didn't see him too often in the summer.

"At the farm again this summer?"

Johnny nods yes.

"Didn't stick your foot in no more cow pies, did ya?" The Kid bent over laughing. Johnny grinned, gave The Kid a shove. When the last bit of licorice disappeared, The Kid slid his tongue over his lips, pondering what to do next.

"Let's go up to the tree." The Kid takes off with Johnny right behind him.

On top of the bluff, straight up from Chuck's store the old oak tree waited. Among the elms and maples, it was something special. It had a mound around its base, as if the good Lord had pulled it up just so boys could lay down on a slant and look at the barges sliding up and down the Mississippi and watch the steam engines a plunking down the railroad tracks going waa, waaa, waaaa as they headed east for Chicago or west to who knows where. In the days before Johnny started going to the farm, the two boys would lay under the old oak tree and waste their sunlight hours talking about this and that or sometimes nothing at all. Now that Johnny was back home and none of his so-called buddies wanted to invest their precious time in The Kid's baseball schemes, he was happy listening to Johnny talk about his recent adventures.

Johnny's house was plunked right on the main drag, which to The Kid was where the action took place. Cattycorner from Johnny's house was a huge empty lot that went a far piece back all the way to the creek. During the summer the gospel tent set up for revival services at night, and Johnny'd sneak over to find out what was happening. This interests The Kid no end.

Johnny declares that the minister is forever hollering and

yelling at the top of his lungs, and saving people all over the place. Says that some of the sinners get so overcome with being saved that they march right up to the front of the congregation and spill their guts about what bad things they have done.

"Right before everybody, Bobby. Can you believe it?"

The Kid marvels at what Johnny is telling him, imagines some of the righteous brethren spurting out who knows what before God and man. There ain't no question in The Kid's thinker that he's missing something big, so he asks who attends these meetings.

"You'll never believe me, but I swear it's the truth -- Mrs. Reeves."

The Kid pops upright and stares at Johnny. Says he'll be switched or something clever like that, because Mrs. Reeves is the meanest old woman that ever walked the face of the earth. Her house is on the corner across the main drag just a block from Johnny's house. She has an apple orchard that she watches day and night waiting for one of the East End wastrels to make a move to appropriate one of her precious apples. Brother, when she spots anybody close to her orchard, she charges out of her house like a banshee threatening to shoot the culprit with her salt and pepper gun. Mrs. Reeves scares The Kid. She was kinda creepy looking and her house is dark, dark, dark. Just the spot Dracula would pick to hole up.

So when Johnny says that Mrs. Reeves is attending the tent meetings, The Kid figures the Lord will nudge her into a spirit of sociability. But Johnny says that the old lady just sits there listening to the minister holler about sinners and evildoers and not changing her sour look one bit. Says her face doesn't even give a flicker when the sinners get down on their knees to confess, which according to Johnny, is about the best darned show in town.

Then last week Johnny claims that Mrs. Reeves speaks to him right nice-like and, get this, even suggests that if Johnny wants an apple he can just waltz into her orchard and get one any old time he wants to. The Kid says this is a miracle for sure. Johnny agrees, but tells The Kid it ain't no religious miracle.

The week after the gospel tent revival meetings, a fast talking healer shows up in the empty lot and pitches his tent. Among the East End high and mighty, Mrs. Reeves shows up and plops herself in the front row. This highbinder informs one and all that if they try a bottle of his elixir, they'll be cured of every ailment known to mankind, from hangnails to high blood pressure. Johnny says that the suckers must like the healer's line of bull because they part with their hard earned cash as fast as they can open up their wallets. Never saw anything like it, Johnny declares.

The topper is that Mrs. Reeves buys a whole box full of the doctor's medicine, and ever since then she has been cured of the means. The Kid says that is darned hard to believe, but Johnny says he will prove it. Down the bluff they scamper.

The Kid climbs up the ladder to the second floor of Johnny's garage that in the old days was a barn. The Kid can tell because it still has a barnyard smell and the hay lying on the floor crackles with age. Johnny dives under a pile of hay and pulls out an empty bottle of elixir he had pilfered from Mrs. Reeves's trashcan. Right there on the bottle it says plain as can be that the elixir will do wonders for the personality, cure those nasty mood swings and that sense of, "goneness," that invades the healthy mind and body. The Kid grabs his throat and rolls around the floor yelling, "help me Johnny, I've got that goneness feeling."

"Okay, Mr. Wise Guy, go on over and visit Mrs. Reeves and it will prove everything I'm telling you."

The Kid ain't too anxious to trot over to the old lady's house because she has threatened him so many times about stealing apples that her mere presence gives him the shakes. But Johnny is so blamed serious about the old woman's change of heart. The Kid feels obligated to show his buddy that he ain't scared.

Johnny's garage/barn has a half door on the second floor that opens out onto the main drag. The boys spot Officer Swen

Larson jawing with Mr. Wenberg on the sidewalk in front of this big signboard across the alley from Johnny's barn. Mr. Wenberg is a backdoor neighbor of Mrs. Reeves and a friend of everybody. Being curious as a couple of sniffing dogs, The Kid and Johnny sneak up behind the signboard and climb up the steel girders.

Usually The Kid uses the signboard as a combination hiding place and observation point from which to direct forays into Mrs. Reeves's orchard, but this time he and Johnny are engaged in a top secret intelligence run the purpose of which is to learn as much as they can about the adult world that controlled their lives.

They overhear Officer Larson telling Mr. Wenberg that the healer who had set up shop in the empty lot is nothing more than a fake who bottles up pure booze and is selling it to the unsuspecting saps as a magic elixir. Officer Larson says that the next time the highbinder shows up, he's going to run him out of town on the rails, and that he's got his eye on Mrs. Reeves as a major buyer.

"Wow," says The Kid, "can you beat that?"

Back in the barn, The Kid and Johnny mull over this turn of events. The Kid claims that if Mrs. Reeves is as nice as Johnny says she is, it's their bounded duty to see that she keeps her supply of elixir. Which is a pretty darned brave statement for The Kid because he's not in any hurry to go out on a limb for the old lady what with Officer Larson lurking in the wings.

Johnny goads The Kid, says go on over and talk to the old woman. The Kid takes in a deep breath and says that's just what he's gonna do. He finds Mrs. Reeves sitting on her front porch with a big smile on her face. When she spies The Kid shuffling along she asks him, nice as pie, how he is doing and how is Ma and the family and would he like a sugar cookie. Just as polite as any normal person can be. The Kid finds his voice and thanks her for the cookie and wishes her a nice day and all that sort of bushwah. When he gets back to Johnny's barn, he says that they sure gotta help Mrs. Reeves because she is as sweet as vanilla ice cream. He puts Officer Larson out of his mind.

Johnny watches the empty lot every night and sure enough, one day the next week, the healer and his wagon filled with magic elixir show up. The Kid tells Ma that he will be down at Johnny's house that evening helping out which is as close to the truth as he can get. The conspirators have their eagle eyes zeroed in on the elixir wagon, and when the healer starts hawking his fakey booze Mrs. Reeves comes a running. The old woman elbows her way through the crowd of sodbusters with manure on their shoes to the front row and waves a handful of bills in the healer's face. In no time at all Mrs. Reeves buys up a whole case of the pleasants and staggers home.

By this time the dimwits are pushing and shoving and waving dollar bills. By golly, nobody is going to miss out on the elixir. The healer is sweating something fierce hauling in the George Washingtons, and he's got a smile on his puss a yard wide. The Kid punches Johnny in the ribs and hoots and hollers, never saw such a terrific show. Then Officer Larson lumbers up and there's a lot of shouting and surly comments about how the local law is interfering with civil rights and all. But Officer Larson stands his ground and threatens to haul the whole sorry bunch downtown unless they get the hell out of there. In the midst of the melee the highbinder packs up his wagon and is last seen heading for the next town.

Next morning The Kid and Johnny are perched on top of the signboard watching Mrs. Reeves's house, and when she appears on her front porch the boys nod to one another. Timing, Johnny says, is everything. Officer Larson, The Kid replies, is whats everything. The plan to save the old lady from her mood swings begins.

The Kid shuffles up to the old woman all pleasant-like, asking about her health and what a fine day it is and other such nonsense. She is in a bit of a haze, but sweet as anything. The old woman insists that he have a sugar cookie that is just a short hop into the kitchen.

"Wait right here, Bobby, and I'll get you one."

The Kid hadn't counted on this turn of events because their plan relied on him keeping Mrs. Reeves busy on the front porch while Johnny lifts her case of magic elixir resting on the back porch. So The Kid starts coughing real loud, and Mrs. Reeves pats him on the back murmuring something about a speedy recovery. Says that maybe a cookie will just "gravitate" The Kid's coughing problem, so why doesn't he have an apple on her instead? The Kid is shaking so much he can hardly get out a proper thank you, but finally he skedaddles leaving Mrs. Reeves rocking on the front porch swing all blissful and happy with the world.

Which gives Johnny the time to liberate the case of fake elixir. Back in the barn the two boys hide the bottles under the straw, then take up their vigil. Sure enough, Officer Larson comes strolling down the alley and heads directly for Mrs. Reeves. They can't hear what he says to her, but he never enters the house and after what seems to be forever he ambles back up the alley with a big grin on his face. Johnny looks at The Kid and The Kid looks at Johnny. They anticipated Officer Larson would search Mrs. Reece's house and confiscate the elixir, but the local law seemed as unconcerned as old Erickson walking on the wing dam.

After Officer Larson disappears, the old lady gets up and walks through her house to the back porch. Suddenly, she comes flying out the back porch door with a wild look in her eye, searching the yard and under the back porch just a shaking her head back and forth and muttering about the unfairness of life. The Kid feels sorry for her, but their plan is only half done.

It is getting on to dark, and once again the conspirators are on surveillance duty in Johnny's barn. They require the cover of darkness otherwise they might be spotted by the law in which case their bodies wouldn't be worth a hoot to anyone. And The Kid is worried about Ma's YOU HOO which is a report home directly threat if there ever was one, and besides the only thing he can get into after dark is, "divelment." But in the cause of serving the greater good, in this case the preservation of a peaceful Mrs. Reeves, The Kid decides to risk Ma's wrath.

He ambles over to Mrs. Reeves's house, and as luck would have it, she's still sitting on the front porch swing. Bold as you please, The Kid asks her how she is feeling. The old lady gives The Kid a bad eye glare, and wants to know why in tarnation he is bothering her. The tone of her voice is just this side of a gallows that The Kid takes quite seriously.

Visions of the old woman pulling out her salt and pepper gun pass through The Kid's mind. How she returned to her old tyrant-self so soon he hadn't a clue, but he sucks 'er up because he has a job to do. After all, Johnny's got the tough job. Boosting that case of elixir onto her back porch takes real daring.

The Kid blathers away about how nice it is to visit one of the kindliest neighbors in the East End and how much he enjoys her cookies and apples. The old lady glowers at The Kid, ordering him off her property, and furthermore, warns him that he has lifted the last apple he's ever going to steal from HER orchard.

The Kid considers her attitude mighty unfriendly, and hightails it around the side of the house. Johnny is tucked behind Mr. Wenberg's garage, and he gives The Kid a thumbs-up signal. As The Kid starts pounding on Mrs. Reeves's back porch door so excited that he almost misses the slam of her front door screen. But he finally unfreezes himself and hightails it, joining Johnny behind Mr. Wenberg's garage.

Well sir, the old lady comes charging out on the back porch to see what all the commotion is, spots the case of elixir, let's out a whoop and grabs a bottle to her bosom. Puffed up with their success the confederates slink across the main drag. The Kid does the hundred-yard dash for home.

Sweating and expecting another lecture about the sins that are committed in the dark, The Kid tiptoes in the kitchen but it's only Sis sitting there. Sis gives The Kid a where have you been look and tells him that Ma is visiting one of the neighbors. The Kid says that maybe he ought to go to bed, and Sis agrees that might be best and for him not to be concerned because Ma'll never know what time he came home. Sis, he decides, is getting sharper by the day.

Lying in bed The Kid congratulates himself. Darned fine plan is what he decides. Figures that for the rest of the summer Mrs. Reeves will be in a right nice mood, a bit hazy maybe, but nice. Darned fine plan, yes sir. Even Prunes and Red would be proud, him taking risks and all. The Kid sleeps with a smirk on his puss that night.

A couple of days later The Kid and Johnny are lazing under the old oak tree and The Kid's saying for the umpteenth time how smart they were and how pleasant Mrs. Reeves seems to be these days, laughing all the time he's talking.

Then Johnny tells him what really happened.

Johnny says that he overheard his Dad talking to Mr. Wenberg about Mrs. Reeves and the magic elixir. Mr. Wenberg relates that Officer Larson just warned her that the elixir was nothing but pure alcohol and wanted her to know that possession of unlicensed booze was illegal, but since he had run the highbinder out of town he wasn't going to pick on Mrs. Reeves for making a honest mistake. Mr. Wenberg claimed that Officer Larson never intended to confiscate Mrs. Reeves's booze.

The Kid ponders this latest bit of news. He and Johnny figured the law was going to grab the old bat's entire stock of elixir, but for crying out loud they had miscalculated, risked their bodies for nothing. Shoot fire, the law was all the time raiding Blackie Cole and carting away his illegal booze, so why didn't they grab the case Mrs. Reeves had?

The question is too deep for The Kid, but the prospect of the elixir making the old witch act like a normal person and not be so trigger happy with her salt and pepper gun sure makes him smile. That blessed gun scares the beegeebers out of a guy, and whether Mrs. Reeves is Dr. Jekyll or Mrs. Hyde means a lot to The Kid's safety.

Course, the apples he lifts from her orchard taste a whole sight better than the ones she deals out free and clear. Now why was that?

The tugs are pushing barges up the river and The Kid can see the tiny figure of Mr. Erickson rowing back to shore with the catch of the day. Johnny is lying with his eyes closed dreaming about how nice it would be to lick an ice cream cone, vanilla or chocolate or tuti-fruti. Johnny opens his eyes and says that he forgot to ask about The Kid's flying experience, says all innocent-like that when he was away at the farm he must have missed the event of the year so why don't The Kid walk him through it.

After what they have been through with Mrs. Reeves The Kid feels he can tell Johnny anything, but just in case Johnny has some sudden inspiration to blab to some loud mouth, The Kid swears Johnny to secrecy.

"Ya, ya, ya, Bobby, Just tell me what happened."

The Kid casts a gander at his buddy and decides to spill his guts. Up under the old oak tree with no prying ears around The Kid talks about how he and Lenny Tremains got into the model airplane building business:

The Kid and Lenny devoured their favorite magazine, *Flying Aces* with rapt attention. In addition to reliving the exploits of *Doc Savage*, The Kid got to studying the ads on model planes. Says he saved up a whole fortune and bought a kit for a World War I Sopwith Camel. Takes patience to build one of those buggers, The Kid claims, but he's diligent as all get out and beyond his wildest dreams the sucker flies.

Sure, it only has a rubber band driven prop, but when Lenny

sees The Kid flying his own homemade creation, he can't wait to get into building one himself. Trouble is Lenny has a problem following instructions not being too coordinated don't you know, and his first model is a pure mess. Kinda all scrunched up, no telling what separated the wings from the tail or the body. So Lenny gets another kit and The Kid helps him cut the balsam strips and glue them to the right form. It ain't exactly perfect because the darned thing nosedives every time Lenny tried to fly 'er.

But he makes progress, and after a few weeks The Kid and Lenny are flying the suckers around and about the neighborhood. They use the empty lot down on 4th avenue and get a kick out of winding up their treasures, and racing smack dab into the main drag after them paying no attention to the chaoogas of the car horns and the swearing of the drivers who near run off the road trying to miss their oblivious bodies. Then the complaints roll in to Ma about how The Kid is just this side of near death. The Kid gets his orders -- find someplace else to become the ace of aces.

One fine day Lenny says, "Let's go up on top the bluff and fly these babies out over 5th avenue."

The Kid considers this a number one idea, and coming from Lenny is remarkable indeed. Up the bluff they go and off the top their planes float in grand style. The suckers hardly make the bottom of the hill let alone 5th avenue, but Lenny and The Kid run up and down watching their models take flight just like they were supposed to do. Making the rat-a-rat-tat sounds of machine guns, they imagine Eddie Rickenbacher shooting down the Red Baron and all those other Huns. Problem was the models crashed dead on the hillside, and after a few flights all they had was broken wings and busted fuselages.

The Kid repaired their Spads and Camels as best he could, but the wings fluttered and the planes plunged to the ground in a twisted heap of balsam and paper. With his own funds being scarce to nonexistent he pleads with Ma for a dime or two to subsidize another model, but she is a wee bit testy every time he works her for anything resembling cold hard cash. The Kid cries a sad tale about how she always supported Prunes in his ventures, and the least she can do will be to deliver a few paltry buffalos to improve the lot of aviation.

Ma allows as how Buddy supported his own tom-fool stunts, and she wasn't in the mood to have her basement filled up with a bunch of worthless planes sitting next to his piles of junk. Translation: Ma's sick and tired of looking at that old diving helmet that just about caused Prunes to be pushing up daises.

The Kid's pleas with Ma fall on deaf ears, and his ears are about bent over from enough self-reliance talks to last him a lifetime. Prunes and Red were useless. They simply stared at The Kid as if he was really brain damaged. Asking for MONEY. No sir, don't spoil The Kid was their motto.

Thankfully, Sis is another matter. Always a soft touch, she coughed up a bit of change without lecturing him to death. When The Kid told her he was on to something big, flying-wise that is, she smiled and opened her purse. If there was any spoiling to do, Sis gladly complied. Sis was the spoiler, and The Kid was the spoilee.

One hot buster in July he gets a sudden burst of inspiration that only comes to a guy once or twice in a lifetime:

"Why don't we have a real dog fight?" he says to Lenny. Just like that, real quick-like, no hesitation, the idea of the century.

"Huh," Lenny mutters.

The Kid explains. In all the movies when the Hun gets shot he waves to the ace-of-aces and goes down in flames, blood dripping from his mouth. Real dramatic-like. Lenny says that's true enough, but what has that got to do with them. The Kid shakes his head. That darn Lenny is a pure trial at times, missing the point faster than you could explain it to him.

The Kid explains to him all careful and slow-like that just before the Red Baron's plane takes off they'll set a match to it, then Eddie Rickenbacher's Sopwith Camel will follow, and smack dab in front of their eyes the hated Hun will crash in flames to his doom. The light goes on in Lenny's eyes and he agrees this could be the biggest thrill of his short life.

The Kid spreads the word among his buddies. For the price of a buffalo, he'll put on a flying show they just can't afford to miss. "Are you nuts?" is their chorus. Getting a bit of loose change out of the whizzer's mitts has about as much probability as the sun setting in the east, so he and Lenny declare that out of the goodness of their hearts, they will put on the extravaganza for free.

The turnout is magnificent. The Kid never considers all the dry grass laying gasping on the hillside, but when the old enthusiasm is running in high gear, who can think of everything?

Besides Lenny complains that he ain't about to be the Red Baron getting shot down in flames and all. Says if he ain't Captain Eddie he's a no show. They argue the fine points for a century or so and finally The Kid gives in, says he'll set a match to his fighter first and let 'er go. Then Lenny follows with his Spad. That Lenny was too dumb to build Rickenbacher's Sopwith Camel, The Kid left unsaid.

"Remember to give out with a bunch of rat-a-tat-tats," The Kid declares. "And when the Red Baron crashes in flames I'll turn to you and give a right smart salute and fall over dead."

Lenny shakes his head as if he understands the script.

"Sounds like a great idea, Bobby, but what really happened?" Johnny has a smirk on his puss The Kid thinks is completely unnecessary. Besides interrupting his story is darned impolite, so he just lays there under the old oak saying nothing, a bit put out if you know what I mean.

"Come on Bobby, I've listened to your model airplane nonsense 'till I'm half groggy, so get on with it." Since Johnny has a few pounds on him, The Kid figures he might as well come clean.

Says he miscalculated something fierce. His plane crashed

in flames just as he had planned, but before he could put on his death scene act, the grass catches fire. Holy smokers, before you can say Jack Robinson, the whole hillside is up in flames. The Kid looks around for his buddies, but the freebies that had yelped and cheered the air battle to end all air battles had disappeared as quick as a covey of quails fleeing the hunter's guns.

Next thing he knows fire trucks and squad car are rounding on the scene. Recovering what wits he had left, The Kid grabs Lenny and they scamper down the hill to 5th avenue. Lenny heads straight for home, but The Kid ain't about to miss out on the fire brigade and all the hoopla. Says he never saw so many adults gather so fast in all his life.

Half the old geezers on life support limp up to partake of a bit of local history. With the firemen and coppers blowing their sirens and sealing off the area, the locals figure the boys-in-blue are out to confiscate Blackie Cole's supply of booze and put the grab on his confederates. The Kid says that he sees Blackie cursing the Young Turks who are taking to the woods like they were shot out of a machine gun. The Kid gets lost in the crowd, but doesn't miss a trick.

The entire hillside was burned to a crisp. The fire chief blamed it on spontaneous combustion, it being so gol-danged hot. Fortunately, they washed the fire out before it got to Blackie's illegal booze otherwise the East End would have had an atom blast only Buck Rogers could deal with.

The Kid has a far-away look in his eyes. Tells Johnny that when you deal with epic air battles you gotta expect the unexpected, to which Johnny raises an eyelid. The more he thinks about it, The Kid says that if he and Lenny could of landed that flaming sucker closer to Blackie's house, what a blast it would have made!

"I think your brothers are right. You really are brain damaged."

Big pause from The Kid, finally says that after things quieted down he gathers up the whizzers and they agreed nobody would squeal about Lenny because he was so young and innocent. The Kid asks them if they are going to blab on him, and they shuffle around and mumble and give him an all-around hard time. Johnny gives The Kid a stare and declares that if it hadn't been for Lenny The Kid would be wearing a striped suit by now.

"What yer Ma have to say?"

"Not a peep," says The Kid.

"Hey, Kid, ya ever smoked?" Innocent-like question from Johnny.

"Sure, plenty of times," The Kid lies. The truth is he tried corn silk wrapped in an old newspaper once and darned near lost his lungs. Remembers coughing like a deranged seal and wheezing like old man Merchins Ought-Nine Dodge. Liked to die on the spot. But The Kid ain't about to admit to Johnny that he's some sort of wimp with cow dung on his shoes.

Johnny claims that he's got part of a pack of Twenty Grands up in the loft above his garage, and that if The Kid is a mind to, he'll scoot on down there and retrieve his smokes.

Ma declared that smoking would stunt his growth, maybe never get any bigger than a pygmy and be all lop-sided to boot. Besides smoking could damage The Kid's brain sure as sin. Each puff and there goes a brain cell according to Ma. The Kid takes this all in and it worries him because every time he does something stupid he gets this brain-damaged business. But he is faced with a question of honor. Anyways, a real cigarette might just be the manly thing to do. So Johnny scampers off for the butts, and The Kid holds the fort trying not to think of a future bumping along like a pygmy.

Like a bad penny -- another one of Ma's sayings -- Johnny puffs up the bluff and tosses the Twenty Grands under the old oak. The Kid takes a cigarette and lights it up tentative-like. Johnny shows The Kid how to inhale and be a real man so The Kid sucks in and the world starts spinning. Around and around it goes, and like this guy on the radio says, "Where it stops, nobody knows." The image of Johnny drifts dream-like in front of him.

Johnny allows to how this is the great life and inquires sweetly if The Kid wants another. The Kid replies that he is trying to cut down, but Johnny insists, says to live 'er up. The Kid ain't too anxious for the pleasure, but once again he lights up and once again he's on his back praying the good Lord will let him walk straight like an average guy. Johnny declares he is out of smokes, but just as soon as he can lay his hands on another pack, he'll sure as shootin' share them with The Kid. Being good buddies and all that.

The Kid produces a weak smile and says how much he appreciates Johnny's generosity.

For a week or so The Kid measures his height to check if he is shrinking up, and he avoids Johnny because he's not all that keen on the smoking bit until he proves for certain smoking won't turn a guy into some idiot whose height ain't going anyplace.

The Kid turns to the absolute authorities who-know-all-there-is-to-know-about-everything-you're-not-supposed-to-do. Asks Prunes and Red about the effects of smoking. Prunes gets a far-away look and says he doesn't know a thing about the evils of smoking. Red puts his arm around The Kid and declares that what Prunes says is absolutely correct. The Kid figures the both of them would rather climb a tree and tell a lie than stand on the ground and tell the truth. They ain't any help at all.

After awhile he forgets the whole sorry matter, figures a guy can't waste his time trying to decide important questions every time he turns around, and besides anything that was fun was somehow bad for you. Lordy, life was trying at times.

That fall with nothing to do and nowhere to go The Kid climbs the bluff and finds Johnny lazing under the tree. Multi-colored leaves cover the ground, crunching as he plunks himself down. It's blustery but sunrays shimmer through the bare branches giving off a shadowy pattern across their bodies.

"Won't be long before it's snowing," says The Kid.

"Ya ain't beating me this year," claims Johnny.

"That'll be the day," challenges The Kid.

"I'm gonna get a new sled for Christmas."

"Won't make a difference. My Flexible Flyer can't be beat."

Johnny says, "What ya want for Christmas?"

Suddenly a curtain drops over The Kid's thinker. He is lost in a time warp all his own He stares at the river, gone on a private trip. They were sitting in the living room, he and Sis eyes glued onto the family album, last Christmas in fact. He spots a picture of Ma from her young lady days in Scotland with a golf club in her hands. He points to the photo and tells Sis about the time he found the golf club bag hanging under the basement stairway filled with old wood shaft clubs so he takes it outside, and in the lawn fronting 5th avenue and the bluff he takes a mighty swipe at a few golf balls the result mighty pathetic. About this time Ma shows up and tees up a ball or two and hits them far and straight across 5th avenue into the alley not quite going up the hill but darn close. He looks on gulping in air like that imbecile Kenny Murchins who is shy a load and slobbers to boot. Ma says that's how to swing not like some gorilla on the loose. Says it will come to him when he grows up. Then she walks off. The Kid's mouth is still taking in the ozone.

Sis admits she didn't know Mom – to Ma she was Mom - could swing a golf club let alone play golf. But then she recalls hearing from a Munro in Chicago that before Mom was married she worked in private golf club. Well Sis says The Kid, all ya'd have to do was see her swing. How'd ya expect the bag and clubs got here? Dad didn't play did he? No says Sis.

"I asked ya what'd ya want for Christmas?" Insistent voice echoing from a tunnel.

But The Kid was still with Sis looking at the family album and the Christmas tree that captivates him. He picked out a photograph of Dad holding him in his arms. He said to Sis, "You knew Dad, but the only thing I know is the dollar bill I get from Grandpa and Aunt Belle at Christmas.

Sis brightens up says that one vacation when they were in Honeyoe Falls, Gramps home in New York, Dad was on the lawn talking to the men and paying no attention to Bud and Jack who were, as usual, yelling and chasing each other. Mom was on the porch half listening to the aunts, but with an eye trained on the rascals. She calls to "Will", that was her name for Dad, more than once, to handle the boys. He ignored her. Finally, to the amusement of the relatives, she charged off the porch, corralled the boys by their respective ears and gave them a what for that was probably heard in Rochester. Mom was embarrassed because at that very time she was trying to make an impression on their Irish Catholic relatives, she being a Scots Presbyterian was an outsider. They even called her Mrs. Glendon, never by her given name, Helen Jemima or, heaven forbid, Dais, like our Munro Clan in Chicago, says Sis.

"I'm asking ya once more, what ya want for Christmas."

Coming out of the trance, The Kid joins Johnny lying under the old oak tree but imagines himself in the living room all warm and toasty on Christmas eve staring at the tree lit up with glittering tinsel.

"A Christmas tree."

"A Christmas tree? That ain't no present."

Silence.

"Ya gotta want something."

The Kid hesitates, shares a secret wish he had never told anybody. "I want my Dad."

The old oak tree was a certainty in The Kid's young life. Guarding the passing scene like a sentinel, its branches opened wide inviting him to share his secrets, never admonishing, never rebuking, timeless as the river it watched over. A breeze whispered gently through its branches and its leaves fluttered to a soft song of secret dreams.

The old oak offered its ageless serenity -- come along boy, lay yourself down and don't worry about a thing.

WHEN 'THE GAME' WAS THE GAME

Ma is at the old pedal-pusher Singer sewing machine making a mackinaw for The Kid from Officer Larson's used great-coat as she had done for Buddy and Jacky. One time one of their pals had gotten a store bought jacket so she went to his mother and asked if she could copy the pattern. The lady said no so

Ma fashioned the boys mackinaws herself. She was an expert seamstress, but the heavy wool tested her resolve. She forced the needle through by hand the old Singer not up to the task. Her efforts saved cold hard cash, and The Kid would be well protected come winter.

The Kid is lolling on the back porch feeling glum if you want to know the truth. He was hoping the iceman would come down the alley delivering ice. When Ma needed ice for the icebox she would put a sign on the back porch signaling she wanted either a 25 or 50 pound chunk. Watching the iceman cut off a chunk with his ice pick the busters would grab slivers of ice as fast as they could grab, then follow him down the alley slurping as they ran behind his wagon. Alleys were The Kid's domain -- playing Kick The Can until dark or shooting hoops through an old iron ring attached to Johnny's garage. He and Johnny were named All Stars on the All-48th Street Alley team. That they picked each other was just luck.

With no iceman in sight the image of a soda pop slipping down his craw takes hold of his thinker so he skedaddles down to Russ's Texaco station wondering if he could finagle good old Russ out of a free soda. That, he decides, had about as much a chance as getting Ma to open her purse, but a guy had to try.

Business is kinda quiet and Russ plops his number tens on his crummy desk, leans back in his chair and asks, "What happened to your eye?"

"Dink Riley slugged me with his bat."

Russ laughs, says, "I didn't know Dink could swing a bat."

The Kid explains that he's on third, there's two outs and Dink, who is still waiting to get the first hit in his miserable life, is up. The Kid figures that the only way they are going to win the game is if he steals home. So he dances around the bag and when the pitcher winds up he takes off arriving at home same time as the ball. Damn Dink swings and nails him just above his left eye which is the last thing he remembers until he arrives home just this side of the loony bin.

Ma inquires what happened and Hooter blathers away about how they had been playing ball down in the empty lot across from Mr. Wenberg's house which ain't too great a place to play ball because it's filled with boulders and holes as deep as the Grand Canyon and pretty darned dangerous to one and all.

Ma grabs The Kid and hustles him inside to perform brain surgery or whatever is close to it. She checks his orbs and they don't seem to be wobbling around too much so she towels off the blood and grabs a few chunks of ice from the ice box and slaps them on his eyebrow. Ma's talking to herself about how last winter he had been carted home after sliding headfirst into a garage, and not a week later he had fallen headfirst off Eko's bike while trying to ride it on the Mississippi that was frozen over, and about the time he came home with his upper lip swollen right out to his nose, and how many injuries can he take to the old noggin?

Russ says with a twinkle in his eye, "You mean you were safe and out at the same time. Or was it out and safe."

Very funny, thinks The Kid.

The Kid tells Russ that Ma is upset no end and cancels his immediate baseball plans so he's been spending his time on the back porch swing listening to the great moments in Cub's history. Sits there with a box of soda crackers and a glass of lime Kool-Aid scoring the games and cheering his hero, Stan Hack, probably the greatest third baseman of all time. The Kid's pretty certain that the success of the Cubs depends on his homemade score sheets made up on a yellow tablet. As he gets caught up in all the excitement, he envisions himself ready for the big leagues when Stan Hack hangs up his glove. But first he has to get a baseball field.

How in the name of Hades can he form the East End Cubs if he don't have a decent field? Russ nods wisely so The Kid marches along before Russ starts hearing the angels.

The older guys at church answer The Kid's problem just like the good Lord intended. The manager of the handle factory down by the railroad tracks allows as to how the church can use the empty field adjoining the factory for a ball diamond, but they'd have to clear the field and keep the weeds cut down.

No problem. The Kid leads his future super stars to the empty lot, and within a day his dream of a real baseball diamond takes shape. It ain't Wrigley Field, but The Kid reasons they ain't in the Bigs either. They play ball day and night. Well, at least up to the time darkness falls and The Kid hears Ma's YOU-HOO. All the players he counted on for his dream-team show up but some of the guys couldn't walk and chew gum at the same time. Duffy and the Cage and Dink Riley were the pits, but The Kid keeps his trap shut for fear of besmirching their non-existent talents. He needed bodies and had to accept the bad with the good. "You see that don't you Russ?"

Russ hates it when The Kid pleads, figures bad news was coming, wishes somebody would drive in for a tank of gas.

It's that darned Dink's fault, The Kid mutters. They were getting in the last innings before the rays disappeared and Dink was at bat. How Dink got that name is a mystery, but The Kid figures that when the Dinker tumbled out of the chute his old man probably yiped, "there's a dink." Jeez, he looked just like a guy called Dink. Kinda small with a head too big for his shoulders and blinkie-like eyes.

Anyway, Dink ain't got the best reputation among the guys because he's forever blabbing to his mother about every last thing the East Enders did. And depending on who had done what, his mother was on the Graham Bell informing the adult world which ended up with one of the good guys confined for the slightest lapse of conduct.

Like cussing. Swearing never went over big with the adults, but The Kid had heard Davey's old man blue up the skies plenty of times so you didn't need to be Sherlock Holmes to figure out where Davey got his mouth. Anyway, Dink wasn't a bad guy, but his mother questioned him every night, probably had a big lamp shining in his eyes ready for the official grilling. After enough of Dink's blabbing about their top-secret operations, the whizzers never included him when they were planning something big.

Problem was that Dink couldn't hit a ball even if he had a tennis racket. The old Dink was about as coordinated as Mary Lou, who by this time, had book ends for arms. The Kid spots Russ wiggling in his chair so he decides he better get to the point quick-like.

The diamond was laid out all regular-like, but they couldn't scrounge up any league-approved equipment, including bases. Russ felt the touch coming, but just yawned which was a sign The Kid was losing him fast. So, The Kid says with his tone up an octave, they used the tops of twenty-gallon drums for bases, and after a summer full of play the lids were bent in the middle, concave shaped. It was getting dark and Dink was up to bat and The Kid was pitching so slow that the ball hung in front of the Dink's eyes for a century or so, and the best the buster could do was a pitiful foul. It's getting darker and darker and everybody is jeering and yelling at him to hit the damn ball.

In the darkness, and unknown to The Kid, Davey sneaks over to second and with his back to the infield pees on the base filling the concave depression with a quart of you-know-what. The Kid hears Davey berating him for not putting the ball in where Dink can hit it. He thinks this is mighty unusual because Davey knows as well as anybody that putting the ball where the Dink can hit is impossible. So The Kid gets up close to the plate and holds the ball squarely in front of the Dink's eyes and orders the buster to hit it, and, by gar, he does. Davey, playing second, makes a fakey half-hearted attempt to field it. Dink heads for first and his excitement soars as he hears Davey and Duffy cheering for him to take two. With the cheers egging him on he legs it for second. Davey plays possum, bends down near the base as if he has a play to make, and at the last moment yells, "SLIDE."

And Dink makes a real professional slide into that peed-up

base. "Holy s...," the Dink yells which is something to hear because the Dink never swears. He gets up sputtering and wiping away at his sloppy pants.

Davey yells something obscene, grabs The Kid, and they hightail it for home. Davey allows as to how this is one of the great gags of his life, but The Kid asks him what in the name of Lucifer does Davey think is going to happen when Dink's mother cross examines him. Davey calls The Kid a spoilsport, says he ain't got a worry in the world. That, The Kid replies, is the most stupid remark he's ever heard.

Russ listens and agrees. He knows Dink's mother.

The next day Ma has the whole sordid story. She runs on about how she doesn't think all that much of the game of baseball, but with the tried and true of the church getting the field she was under the belief The Kid was doing the Lord's work and here she has to listen to some seamy tale that involves her youngest, and what kind of rascals is he running with anyway? And if that isn't enough Mamie Epperson reports he's been dodging her poetry lessons and if that's the case he can just forget baseball so make tracks young man for Mamie's house straight away. Lordy, The Kid asks Russ, what's the world coming to?

Russ shakes his head as if he's agreeing with Ma, which doesn't set so well with The Kid. Jeez, a guy can't trust any adult. It's us against them, no question about it.

By unanimous agreement, the East End elders decree the baseball field off limits for a period to be determined which, according to The Kid, probably means until he is riper than old man Jakes who gets pushed around in a wheel chair and must be close to a hundred. He waits to get a sign of sympathy of sorts from Russ, but Russ's eyes have glazed over and he's close to a snore or two.

But that doesn't stop The Kid. With the ball yard off-limits, the whizzers are out in front of Duffy's house not doing much of anything at all, just a nutsin' around, getting caught up in

Superman and *Batman*. They decide their parents have some sort of conspiracy going on just because of a little peeing incident, but mostly they blame Dink because he can't keep his trap shut. Fact is, nobody's seen Dink for a couple of days.

Davey starts in again on Dink, says that the first time he sees the squealer, he'll clean the whizzer's clock, but Duffy claims that Dink's mother likely has his worthless body trussed up in the basement so he won't get contaminated by no wisenheimer like Davey who is so uncivilized he uses second base instead of a bathroom to perform his daily duty. Davey doesn't take kindly to Duffy's remarks so he chases his buddy around the yard a time or two. Finally they both run out of gas and slump down glaring at each other which is kinda dumb when you think about it because the real culprit, Dink, is probably in the movie house watching *Tom Mix* or *Lash Larue*, and getting cool. The rascals sit some more and stare some more, and do nothing at all some more.

About this time, The Kid informs Russ, he gets a flash of inspiration. Russ groans, but before The Kid has a chance to continue a right smart Model A drives into the station.

Russ jumps up and puts on his smile of the month and jabbers away while filling up this damsel's pride and joy. While Russ is laying it on thick about what a terrific car she has, The Kid wonders how much he oughta tell Russ. Finally, Russ whistles his way to the cash register and plunks down a George Washington that makes him one happy man. Of course any skirt makes Russ one happy man, but that's beside the point. The Kid smiles at good old Russ with a you gotta hear the rest of my story so Russ plunks himself back down.

Well sir, there's these old boxing gloves hanging up in the basement, and just like that, yipes The Kid, inspiration flashes through his noggin. "What about a boxing tournament?" says he to the assembled busters. Davey and Duffy brag about how they would just love to get Dink Riley in the ring for a good old-fashioned pounding, but The Kid quashes that idea as being unfair to the uncoordinated. Besides, we been scratched from playing ball for watering up second base what do you think would happen if he came home all bloodied up. Forget Dink.

The Kid races home to get the gloves that have been hanging on a nail in the basement for a couple decades, covered with cob webs and crummy with dust. Meanwhile Duffy runs some rope around the trees in his front yard and the boxing ring takes shape, sort of. The Cage lifts a tin pie plate and an iron ladle from his Ma's kitchen, and offers to bang the rounds in and out. The Kid holds a tin can to his mouth and announces that the first matches of the East End Boxing Club will begin.

There wasn't exactly a mad rush to put on the gloves, so lots were drawn and The Kid and Duffy lose. "Rules," Duffy declares, "we gotta have rules or I won't fight. And I want a second that can count to ten." Sure. "And no more than three rounds." Okay. "And The Kid's second better have a white towel so he can stop the fight before he gets killed."

Duffy's got a smirk on his face that The Kid don't cotton to. The guys are yelling for blood, anybody's blood but their own. Start fighting and quit talking for crying out loud or words to that effect.

Once in the ring, Cage plunks the pie tin and the contestants shuffle toward each other. The Kid gives it the old soft shoe, dances around throwing fake punches like Kid Dempsey who won the Golden Gloves in the big city. Duffy just stands there doing nothing at all, his big mouth closed, not too enthused about the whole thing if you want to know the truth. With nothing going on but The Kid bobbing and weaving the boos start and the guys get restless.

It was embarrassing, so The Kid throws a pretty good one two that bounces off Duffy's body. Duffy backs up and bends over holding his stomach with a hurt look on his puss, not defending himself or anything. His seconds throw in the towel and the Cage declares The Kid the winner and champpeeeen.

Duffy accuses The Kid of throwing illegal punches, and a shouting match begins between The Kid's and Duffy's seconds which don't amount to much since none of the whizzers are willing to put up their dukes. Anyway, on the scene appears Mickey the Mope who is older and bigger than the wisenheimers, and a bit out of his usual territory thinks The Kid. This Mick ain't like Billy Gee who ain't had a successful day unless he's pounded the pee outta some undersized shaver. But Mick ain't exactly a pleasant sight either because he's got a rep as tough guy.

Russ is about to nod off because by this time he's getting bored with The Kid's story, but being a good guy and all he fights his eyelids open especially when he hears the name Micky which is no good by Russ's standards because he's got the eye on him for lifting a few of his tires which he can't prove but wishes he could.

The Kid notes Russ's mind wandering, but he goes along with his story that he knows is pretty darned good if Russ will just pay attention.

The wisenheimers take a gander at Mickey and start to shuffle their sneakers for a fast getaway. Cage boasts about how The Kid was the champeeeen of the East End having just whipped the beejeebers out of Duffy who, as you can see, is holding his sides from the brutal pounding The Kid gave him.

The Mick gives The Kid an awful stare and asks him sweet-like if he'd mind getting in the ring with him since he's the reigning champeeeen and all. Suddenly The Kid ain't feeling too well, but there weren't any graceful way to back out and besides Duffy's big mouth is yapping away about how The Kid is a terrific body puncher and how Duffy held The Kid off long as he could but the East End slugger is just plain tough.

The Kid figures Duffy is giving him a payback, but he's mighty upset with all the other guys praising his fighting talents just to save their own worthless skins. It don't take a Dr. I.Q.

to figure out that if somebody is going to get pounded, they'd cough up The Kid to protect their own miserable hides.

"What do you think about them apples Russ?" Russ shrugs his shoulders as if to say get on with it.

The Kid decides that if he was to ensure his secret desire to manage the East End Cubs, he'd better get into the ring. Leadership and all. When the Cage rings the gong for round one the Mick fairly leaps out of his corner and The Kid starts his shuffling routine, circling Mickey the Mope who has a real mean look on his puss. Like some old bull in season, the Mick starts throwing punches and The Kid's feet shuffle faster and faster. Suddenly, he failed to duck and The Kid is laying flat on his back.

"I'll be darned," The Kid says to himself. Shoot fire, he got hit but it didn't hurt all that much. His seconds were posed to throw in the towel, but The Kid jumps back up. And gets knocked down again. And gets up. And gets knocked down again. The Kid gets in a few punches, but is so busy avoiding Mick's fists that it all becomes a bit hazy. He remembers hearing the gong, but he's about in never-never land when the Cage pronounces the fight over.

Mickey helps The Kid to his feet and asks if he's okay, says he's sorry if he really hurt him. The Kid gives off with a feeble smile, and the busters are saying what a grand fight he put up.

When he gets home Ma takes a gander at The Kid and wonders how long he is going to last if every time he comes in the door he's got some head injury. "How did it happen?" Ma asks while applying a sliver of ice to his left eye that by now is puffing up. She asks, a bit sharply he thinks, who gave him permission to use the old boxing gloves, and when he just shrugs she informs him that she declared the gloves off limits after the time Buddy beat the stuffing out of Jacky when they were shavers. Seems Dad had brought the gloves home so as to teach Buddy and Jacky the fine art of boxing, an experiment that lasted all of one round.

Then Ma changes her tune all tender-like since The Kid is hurting and she isn't the kind to pick on a guy when he's down. She orders The Kid to stop all this nonsense, or else. The Kid ain't so stupid he don't know what Ma's or else means, so the old gloves join the East End Boxing Club in the annals of sports history.

"Did ya hear about the Boy Scout troop?" As if to head The Kid off, Russ says that he kinda heard something along those lines. The Kid ignores Russ's lackadaisical attitude and plows ahead.

Seems the parents put the arm on Mr. Graves, the local shop teacher, telling him they would appreciate it if he would exercise his control over the rascals, and what about it if he started a Boy Scout troop? Mr. Graves is enjoying his summer of respite, free and clear of the wiseacres, but the pressure is terrific. He isn't too thrilled with the request, nay demand, but agrees to open McKinley school up in the evening to teach the boys standards of conduct and all that bushwah.

When Ma tells The Kid what awaits him, he's mighty excited, figures the scouts will be a first class experience. Ma contends that The Kid will be getting an extra helping of Christian brotherhood even though the meetings will be held in the evening. It stretched her, "divelment after dark," decree, but she was sick and tired of listening to him moan about the baseball field.

By this time Russ is snoring away in his chair, but The Kid figures if he talks loud enough Russ will get the point. A breeze is wafting through the garage doors and the station is quiet. The Kid wonders if Russ would mind if he had a cream soda. He sidles up to the cooler, lifts the lid and scans the sodas. Then he closes the lid slowly and returns to his seat empty-handed. The Kid doesn't catch Russ's half-slit eyes watch him. Nor the brief grin that passes over Russ's puss.

Having been given the job of forming the first ever East

End Boy Scout Troop, Mr. Graves takes his marching orders seriously. Every walking boy body is invited to participate, democracy being the in thing. Along with the East End Baseball Dream Team, who shows up but Dink Riley. The Dinker has been pretty scarce since that little problem he had when he slid into second base. This was the first time Dink had been face to face with the busters, and he's mighty quiet sitting by himself in the back row.

Mr. Graves is zooming along with the Boy Scout oath and what it means to be a scout and all the good deeds they would do for the community that sounds wonderful, but nothing was happening. The critters sit in McKinley's gym looking at the baskets, wondering when they were going to shoot some hoops, but the old Graves walked them through the Boy Scout paces like they were a bunch of slow wits or something.

The Kid gets restless and decides to go to the washroom that is on the other side of the locker room. The locker room must have absorbed the sound because when The Kid walks in the washroom he hears Dink Riley screaming and blubbering something awful. Davey and Duffy got the sucker's head in one of the toilets flushing away and yelling at the top of their lungs that Dink is a no good squealer who can't be trusted with the time of day.

Russ pops up out of his revere and inquires, "What in tarnation is wrong with you busters?" The Kid's got a grin a yard wide, figures if this story doesn't earn him a soda, nothing will. So on he goes.

Davey yells at The Kid to join them, declaring they'll give that damn Riley a lesson he won't soon forget. The Kid stands there all bug-eyed, considers Davey's methods a wee bit extreme, but what the hey, may as well join in on the fun.

"What the hell is going on in here?" Mr. Graves is screaming out some A-Number One cuss words, but he catches himself and deposits his eyes on Dink. Like a beached whale, Dink is gulping in these big slugs of air and spewing out streams of water all at the same time.

The Graves quiets down a bit and asks Dink how he feels and what is going on and such. Dink casts a sideways glance at Davey and Duffy, declaring he lost a dime in the toilet and his "friends" were just helping him retrieve his fortune. Everybody stares at Dink in disbelief. Mr. Graves stands there huffing and puffing, ready to hang Davey and Duffy and The Kid up by their thumbs and his star witness, as innocent as can be says, "They were just helping me, Mr. Graves."

By this time the entire troop is hanging around the washroom watching the scout leader attempt to discover some sort reason in this insanity. He informs Dink that if he hadn't appeared on the scene one Dink Riley would be history by now. But Dink just smiles. Then Graves belabors The Kid for standing there like a dunce, not even calling for help. Pitiful example of a Boy Scout, he yells.

Exasperated, Mr. Graves runs the troop back to the gym and begins trial proceedings.

He blathers away about whether his charges should be dismissed for the good of the troop, but spying Dink happy as a dog with Davey's and Duffy's arms around him all palsy-walsy, he's so confused he announces that justice will be meted out at the next meeting.

With that the busters laugh and yell and bounce around. Their conduct, or lack thereof, so infuriates Mr. Graves that he thunders the troop to be quiet and announces solemnly that Davey and Duffy are hereby dismissed from the troop for conduct detrimental to scouting. Then the gym teacher turns to The Kid and says that he will exact his punishment at the next meeting. The Kid never saw a man so mad in all his life, figured that he better skedaddle out of there while he still had his skin.

Just then Dink speaks up loud and clear. Says that if his "good buddies" are being dismissed, he might as well be cashiered too since he could never belong to a troop without them.

The Kid's stunned. Not ten minutes before Davey and Duffy are trying to drown the Dink, and now they are, "good buddies." The enemies-turned-chums cast a fish eye at him so The Kid allows as to how sorry he is about this misunderstanding and all, but if it is the same to Mr. Graves, he'd just as soon stay home next week. The shop teacher turned Boy Scout leader waves his arms in disgust and walks out.

On the way home Dink and Davey and Duffy are telling one another what great guys they are, which is a mite sickening to the ear. Dink's house is the first one on the way so The Kid asks him what he's gonna tell his mother, decides Dink'd better have a story worked out before his mother puts him under the lamp giving him the third degree.

Dink looks at The Kid with an innocent smile and says he's gotta tell the truth. The Kid is aghast. The last time Dink tells the truth they lost their baseball field, and now with him darned near needing a pulmotor to save his worthless body, The Kid figures he'll be locked up for life.

Yah," Dink says, "I'll tell my Mom that I can't afford to take so much time away from my studies so I quit the troop."

Everybody busts out laughing and slapping one another on the back because Dink and books are about as far apart as the north and south poles. His mother was forever moaning about his poor grades. Smirking to himself, The Kid tells Dink to come down to the house and he'll give him a keen book of poetry which he received free and clear from none other than Mamie Epperson and he can carry it around for looks if nothing else.

"Poems?" the Dinker moans.

"That's sissy stuff," claims Duffy.

With that Davey slaps The Kid on the back, asks him sweetly if he has one for him, too, and the trio of misfits bend over laughing and pounding one another.

The Kid curses under his breath. Figures this was a great chance to pass off Mamie Epperson's *SUNBEAMS* with none the wiser, but his buddies queer the deal. So he promises Dink his geography book that weighs a ton and a half and will impress his mother no end.

"And you mean this works?" Russ asks eyebrows up like The Kid's been smoking corn silk again.

"Sure as shooting," says The Kid. "I got the Dink to memorize where Chicago is, you know something that don't tax his feeble mind, and his mother is pleased no end. Fact is, she's so pleased with Dink's progress she talks Ma into raising the baseball ban. What about that?"

Waiting for a response The Kid stares at the gas station owner, but Russ just yawns and rubs the sand out of his eyes. Jeez, The Kid hopes that Russ didn't miss any of his story because he's still feeling down, and for crying out loud if Russ ain't about to give him a boost, who will?

Russ is waiting to pounce on the next bohunk that drives into his station, but the prospects for such an event are growing dimmer by the minute. Russ smiles and scrunches his rump further down in his chair, says to The Kid's sourpuss, "Look at it this way, if you're back in the old ball yard what's the beef? Wait a sec, don't tell me you caught another bat on yer noggin?"

"Well," says The Kid, "something like that."

"What'd yer mother say?"

"If you let me finish, I'll tell ya."

"Keep it short."

Russ's gotta point, but he ain't got the whole story, which will grab Russ's interest no end. Seems that The Kid finds a baseball nut named Herbie down at Riverside Park hitting ground balls to a bunch of aces that throw at ought miles an hour which occurs to The Kid he's just found easy pickings. After a little of this and a little of that with Herbie they form a league. Herbie, who has glasses an inch thick, is a St. Louis Cardinal fan, but otherwise an okay guy. They shake hands and The Kid heads home to round up the East End Cubs.

From first to third, Davey, H, Hooter and The Kid know what's happening, but with Dink and Duffy in the outfield The Kid prays for help. Johnny is okay, but he can't play the entire outfield by himself. Cage's old man gets some beat up catching gear, so naturally, Cage put on the tools of ignorance and became the Cubs first string catcher. Behind home plate Cage looked like a character out of *Buck Rogers*, kinda spacey if you want to know the truth. Jonesy pitched. He had a decent fastball and a slow curve that was a beauty. Sort of bent the ball over the plate in the same degree his right arm was bent. You could smell Jonesy a block away because he poured Sloan's liniment by the bottle full on his slightly deformed arm. But he could throw, no mistake about that.

The Kid faces his first managerial decision when Davey, a top-flight first baseman, demands to be an outfielder. "Wanna be with Dink and Duffy," Davey insists. The Kid argues but Davey says he'd quit if The Kid don't put him out there next to his true-blue buddies.

If he had signed contracts like they had in the Bigs, The Kid would be able to order Davey around, but since Davey had no contract The Kid backs down, tells himself it was in the best interests of the team, puts Johnny on first. He wonders if all managers are cowards at heart. Brother, this wouldn't happen in the Bigs.

If Duffy was awful, Dink was even worse. After the ten zillionth fly ball hit to him, Dink had yet to catch one. If the fly went long he'd run in, and if the ball went short he'd run out. Dink runs around in circles yelling, "I got it, I got it," but never making the connection. The Kid is getting mighty depressed. He shakes the bushes for another player, but finally has to admit that he's stuck with Dink and Duffy.

Otherwise, The Kid's darned pleased with himself. He's the manager. What an honor his teammates had bestowed on him.

He never considered it work to make up the schedules, set the rules for league play, make out the line-up cards, tend to the equipment, that is, carry all the balls and bats, and find time to argue with the prima-donnas who sulked about the unfairness of the batting order.

Ma gives him a good what for one fine day as he was about to embark for the big game all loaded down. Seems to me, she says none to sweetly, some of the other clowns could help out. Ma just didn't understand. The Kid was THE MANAGER, and the guys counted on him to carry out all the sacred duties associated with running a first-class team. That's what The Kid thinks, anyway.

It didn't take too long to figure out that Dink and Duffy weren't working out. Not only were the East End Cubs losing games, but The Kid's reputation is going down the drain. Opposing players fall all over themselves with laughter when Dink and Duffy play certain outs into doubles. Jonesy's arm is getting benter and benter from throwing so many curve balls. If he don't get a strike out or induce a grounder, the game is all but over.

Anything to center and right is a double or even a home run. One day a fly ball falls between Dink and Duffy and they near kicked the ball into the next county. Jonesy strikes out the next three batters because their eyes were so misty from watching the pathetic outfield play they couldn't see the ball. It was humiliating.

The Kid's getting more despondent game by game. The East End Cubs are the laughing stock of the league. No matter how much practice the dumbbells had, Dink and Duffy still kicked the ball around, and if they were fortunate enough to get their mitts on the ball they threw it to the wrong base. The Kid bingos onto a great light-bulb idea. There hadn't been any inner-league trades yet, so he approaches Herby and the Cardinal manager says inner-league trades sound okay to him.

The Cardinals got a southpaw by the name of Big Jim Terry

who could really smoke the ball. He's the fastest thrower in the league. But wild. Big Jim either strikes out the side or walks a zillion guys across the plate. In Jim Terry, The Kid sees nothing but potential with a capital P. Imagining Big Jim pitching alongside of Jonesy, The Kid lays awake nights conspiring how he would make the trade.

The next game with the Cardinals is tied up in the seventh. With two outs, Billy Thomas, the Cardinals free swinger, is up at bat with runners on first and third. Jonesy throws a beauty of a curve and Thomas strikes out. Disgusted, he heaves the bat for all it's worth. Just then The Kid comes charging off the field with his head turned toward the outfield waving Dink and Duffy in, wondering to himself if these two beauts will ever catch up to the fact that after three outs the sides change.

As he turns around Billy Thomas's bat catches him in square in the chest. The Kid drops with a thud, knocked out cold, once again listening to the birds chirping away. When he comes to Billy Thomas's dead white face hovers over The Kid swearing that he will never again throw a bat in anger, a most unlikely event because Thomas has a temper known far and wide.

Still on his back The Kid wonders, to the amazement of the assembled players, who drove the truck through the diamond.

"He's talking!" yipes Billy Thomas.

"Better get him home," yells, Herbie.

Hooter says, "Not me, I ain't facing his Ma again."

Dittos come from the rest of the East End whizzers. A mite wobbly The Kid struggles to his feet says to Herbie that he wants a talk after the game is over. Although his chest hurts like the devil he senses that he's got Herbie in a corner. Big Jim Terry is so upset he walks in a zillion runs and the East End Cubs win the game. Hooter hauls the equipment home.

A toot from the gas pumps jars Russ out of his revere, and he trots out to do some serious cash business. Which gives The

Kid time to slosh down a swig of water from a water jug that Russ has stashed in the cooler. As Russ plops a couple of coins into the cash register The Kid wonders out loud if Russ is ready for the rest of the story.

"You mean there's more?"

The Kid nods, picks it right up.

Herbie agrees to make the trade. Jeez, with The Kid getting clunked in the chest what choice does he have? Big Jim Terry for Dink Riley straight up, but the Cardinal Side manager refuses to take Duffy even as a throw in. No way does he want two misfits. So the deal is made and The Kid staggers home, figures a little Andy Lotshaw's liniment, bottled by the Cub's trainer, will make him feel right as rain.

Next day at the ball diamond down by the handle factory, The Kid gets the team together for practice and an old pep talk and says what a great win it was over the Cardinals. When everybody is congratulating each other he sneaks in how he traded Dink for Big Jim Terry. The team is astounded.

Jim Terry for their good buddy and all-around terrific center fielder. This stops The Kid dead. Is he hearing right? These busters do nothing but blame Dink for losing game after game, and now they liken him to the great Cub outfielder, Augie Galan.

The Kid senses that he is up against it so he gives them a run down: Dink has yet to catch a fly ball, and worse yet he has never put the bat on the ball, and besides somebody has to make the tough decisions which is what managers are for. Davey allows as to how The Kid broke up an all-star outfield for a smokin' wild man who is crazy like all southpaws are. Practice is over.

The Kid works with Big Jim's control, tells him to shorten his kick and bend his back. Work to the catcher's mitt, for crying out loud! After five minutes of Terry's wild ones, the Cage throws down his mitt, declares that no way is he going to put his body in front that fast ball. Hooter sees The Kid's problem and volunteers to catch the crazy lefty which means The Kid has to switch players to new positions which heats up the air no little bit. As he watches Cage attempt to catch a fly ball he thinks maybe he should have kept old Dink because Cage, for all his work behind the plate, falls over his feet in the outfield. Morale ain't worth a darn.

The next game finds Dink playing right field for the enemy that eases The Kid's mind knowing the buster was a first class screw up. Big Jim assures The Kid that he will strike out every last Cardinal. The game's in the bag, he says. But Big Jim walks batter after batter and the Cardinals' smirk their way around the bases. The Cubs are losing a zillion to nothing and the East End bench gets grimmer and grimmer.

Then with Cub's runners in scoring position, The Kid laces a deep fly to right, a sure hit, but Dink hauls it in, yells something like put this where it hurts. As the game goes on -- endlessly goes on -- The Kid's last bit of sanity departs on the four o'clock freight. Dink grabs not one but two fly balls which is two more than he made for the East End Cubs. And he gets the walk off the wild one that wins the game for the Cardinals. To add to The Kid's embarrassment Cage drops everything hit to him, complains that the manager has him out of position. The Kid is in a state of shock.

After the game Davey calls a team meeting. Duffy allows that since The Kid was felled with Thomas's bat he ain't thinking too straight. He's ruining a championship team, Duffy charges. Even Davey nods yes. The Kid is fired and Hooter takes over as manager. While this confab is going on, Dink is waiting to walk home with Davey and Duffy. Dink sticks it to The Kid, says he is willing to instruct the Cage how to play the outfield, yuk, yuk, yuk.

The Kid arrives home dejected. Fired before his career ever gets a chance to bloom. Ma notices him sitting quiet-like at the supper table and asks what is wrong and he spills his guts.

"Bobby, you must look on the bright side of things," Ma says.

The Kid ain't in the mood for a silver lining lecture and he asks Ma what possibly could be bright about getting fired from the job of a lifetime.

"Look at it this way, son. You don't have to carry all that equipment anymore."

Sitting in one of Russ's old greasy chairs and blabbing out his life's story didn't seem to help at all. Gosh darn it, his best buddies turning on him that way hurt. That stupid Dink's like an anchor around his neck, ruining every great plan The Kid comes up with. If it hadn't been for Dink he'd never been barred from the baseball field, he'd still be a Boy Scout, and he'd still have the greatest job in baseball. Dink sticks in his throat like one of Ma's dumplings. He'd done the best he could for the team, trading Dink for a loony left-hander was just this side of genius. But it hadn't turned out that way. No sir, bet your boots on that.

Shoot fire, was all this conspiring worth it? The Kid raises his eyes, pleading for an answer, but Russ is stretched out in his chair, his legs crossed on the edge of desk, peepers closed. Jeez, The Kid wanted some of Russ's sage adult thinking, needed help figuring out what to do.

Then visions of a cream soda crosses The Kid's thinker, and he pads softly to the cooler. He raises the lid quietly, wondering if he dares take one without permission. The temptation is overwhelming. With the soda in hand, the former manager of the East End Cubs sits down and takes a pull, smacks his lips, hoping Russ won't be too mad at him.

Through slit eyelids Russ follows The Kid and smiles. The Kid is okay. A little dense at times, but okay.

A MATTER OF HONOR

Jack, Cully Johnson, Soup Tisdale and Swede's dog

Red's the kinda guy who makes everybody happy. If you don't smile when Red casts his grin around, you gotta be hard-hearted indeed. Ma's number two son is a confirmed devil through and through. You can see it in his eyes. And though he hates school and books and regular type learning, he's sharp and keen-witted and one step ahead of just about everybody. When Red tells a story, and he has plenty of stories to tell, his audience, whether one or several, break up with his antics. When The Kid was a shaver he and Ma would stand by the kitchen window and watch Red on his way to school goofing around, acting like he was running into a tree, that sort of nonsense. He gives Ma and The Kid a big laugh to start their days.

During those languid days of summer when the sun was up Red was usually found under the backyard elm nutsin' around with his bicycle. He was a born tinkerer, loved to take things apart and put them back together. The new departure brakes on his bike were worn thin from his madness for perfection. He spent hours cleaning and greasing the parts and reassembling them just so. The wheels were fine-tuned to produce the ultimate speed possible.

From the back porch swing The Kid catches Red's self-satisfied look and knows he's about to take that sucker out for a test run. Up 48th Street hill and peddling down to his utmost was his favorite run. Red and his tests were predictable.

The Kid returns his attention to the radio broadcast of the Cub game. This occurs about the time a broadcaster named Ronald Reagan is airing a ticker tape play by play from station WOC in Davenport, Iowa. As Reagan thrills The Kid with hits, runs, and errors he barely notices Ma unpinning the laundry from the clothesline that runs across the backyard.

Holding a basket filled with laundry Ma is opening the back door just as Red comes racing into the yard. Eyes misting from the rushing wind he never sees the clothesline. His victory cheer turns into a shriek as his neck catches the line. The Kid yelps as he spots his brother suspended in mid-air, the riderless bike staggers along like Blackie Cole carrying a full load.

Ma screams, "Jacky," drops her basket and runs.

Gasping for breath, Red lays on the ground clutching his

throat. His words gurgle out, unintelligible, pathetic. A nasty scarlet line runs from ear to ear, tears flow from his eyes. With Ma comforting him, The Kids backs away slowly. Ma administers Vaseline to the offending injury, her beloved Jacky sounds like a frog croaking on a lily pad.

The speed demon of the East End slowly picks up his bike whose front wheel that minutes before had the balance of a fine Swiss watch now wobbles along like old man Gaines struggling with his cane. Red upends the Bike and unscrews the axle bolts. Faced with Red's determination The Kid stands off not knowing exactly what to say. But he knows one thing for sure. Red'll have that sucker running faster than the wind, but you can cross out the backyard as the finishing line.

As he returns to the back porch and the Cubs he spots Ma taking down the clothesline muttering to herself.

One fine summer morn Ma announces that from that day forward The Boys will be in charge of the weekly shopping downtown. Says their education will not be complete without this practical learning process that will make men of them.

Red peers at the ceiling, knows that from here to eternity his Saturday mornings are shot. Briefly, he considers making an objection to the high court judge, but when Ma's mind is set nothing can change it. The Boys make some grumbling noises, but they nix it considering their bones are too precious to place in jeopardy.

Ma gives them the old, "Boy's If I Could Do It, I'd Do It Myself," and a few other selected homilies taken from her Good Book of Raising Malcontents. The Kid listens to these one-way exchanges seriously because he suspects that one day he, too, will become the Saturday morning shopper.

Ma scours the Friday newspaper that lists all the good deals, food-wise. Then she considers what is and what is not necessary to preserve life, and opens her purse - which is no mean feat - to find the exact amount required to fend off starvation in the old homestead. Down to the EXACT penny, mind you. Ma is so used to scrimping and saving every nickel that she isn't truly happy unless the old buffalo screams before it departs her clutches.

Armed with her list and sufficient hard currency to bring back a bag of vittles, The Boys begin their weekly trips downtown to do battle with the local merchants.

Red's a master flimflam artist, an in-born force which he gives vent to at all times and in all places. Each encounter with this or that clerk tests his inherent ability to practice the arts of deception. He works the downtown stores quickly, but with his eyes open. Is there an advantage to be gained? If so, how can he pull it off?

One autumn Saturday he is standing at the meat counter of the A&P deciding which piece of ham looked the best. He points to a right nice piece and tells the butcher he'll have 25 cents worth. The butcher cuts off a slice, weighs it, says it will cost Red 30 cents. As Ma only allows him 25 cents for the ham, Red stands firm, says he'll pay 25 cents, not a penny more. The butcher is upset with the red head that is holding up the cash-on-the-barrel-head customers who just might disappear across the street to his major competitor. So, ornery-like, he whacks the slice nearly in half, slaps one piece on the scale and announces it will cost Red 25 cents. Red loves it. Anybody simple enough to try to cheat the old red head is just down his alley.

Red informs the butcher that if it's all the same he'll take the piece laying on the butcher block for the five-cent difference. The butcher starts to lay into Red something awful, but Red says loud and clear that Ma's home with a terrible disease and she don't know how she's gonna feed her brood and she has to pinch her pennies so hard she's coming down with arthritis of the fingers and, blah, blah, blah.

The lady customers are mighty taken with Red being such a wonderful son and all, and they glare at the butcher who has the compassion of a telephone pole. Red gets the five-cent piece of ham that, don't you know, is the same size as the 25-cent piece, and off he goes to do battle with some other slicker who wants to match wits with the master. Can't wait to tell Ma.

Ma never gives The Boys carfare, doesn't intend to dip into the treasury for such foolishness. Besides, Ma contends that hitchhiking rides downtown and back will build their character. Truth is, Ma uses the carfare money for food. All the baloney about building character is just her Scottish heritage rising to the occasion.

So, Prunes and Red hitchhike. Getting a ride downtown ain't any great shakes, but thumbing a ride home with an armful of groceries is another matter. It don't take Red long to figure out that when motorists spy two wastrels burdened down with grocery sacks, they push down on the gas pedal and pass them by without so much as a howdy do.

Red uses all eight cylinders and comes up with a solution. After he and Prunes work the local merchants they meet behind a big signboard on the edge of downtown. Prunes hides behind the signboard with the grocery sacks while Red casts his smile about for a fish dumb enough to grab his hook. When the unsuspecting motorist stops, Red opens the car door and Prunes busts out from behind the signboard like Bronco Nagurski crashing through the line.

While the startled motorist watches Prunes heave the groceries in the back seat, Red gabs away about how the devil his brother got there is beyond him, but he can't leave him now can he - Sir? Then Red and Prunes jump in and Red inquires all sweet-like if the motorist will please let them off in the East End. What could the poor sap say?

The downtown merchants can handle Prunes, but the general opinion is that, in a crowd of women customers, Red's too much for them. Red has a way of turning the crowd to his advantage, tales of his suffering mother just this side of death's door brings tears to the dear lady's eyes. Why wouldn't the storeowner sell

Red this or that at a reduced price, they demand? Drastic action, the merchants decide, is required.

In this equation of Ma's teenage hustlers, Prunes is not exactly an unknown quantity to the downtown merchants. One particularly exasperating Saturday the manager of the New York Store gets Prunes aside and asks him if he wants a job, figuring he'd rather have Prunes inside the tent where he can watch him rather than outside disrupting his cash sales.

Work? Sounds okay to Prunes. Sure beats topping onions in the sweltering heat at ten cents a bushel, or so he thinks. What he gets ain't precisely what he had bargained for – all the hard work, lifting, hauling, pushing, grunting, all the time in the basement lit by dim 20 watt bulb, listening to a gruff voice from above ordering him to bring up a sack of this or a giant box of that. AND RIGHT NOW!

Two weeks into the New York Store's pits Prunes decides he has heard his last command. That scudder of a manager just won't let up. If he doesn't get out of the dungeon soon he'll end up with a broken back. Which makes him take a long hard gander at his situation. One more Saturday in the midnight cellar hoisting hundred pound sacks will break him for sure. He knows he can't just quit because Ma'd have him lynched at dawn, and bailing out of a paying job in Ma's eyes is the sin of all sins. According to Ma's theory of survival ten cents an hour is a whole lot better than no cents an hour.

But what if he's fired? . . . Yes sir, if he takes the long count he'll be able to place the blame on the store manager, tell Ma he'd tried his darndest but he had been done in by a stupid accident that was no fault of his own. There were times, Prunes decides, when his own brilliance was just too much.

The next Saturday he puts his plan into action. Staggering up the stairs from the basement from hell he drops a hundred pound bag, and suddenly a cascade of white beans rain down the steps like pebbles falling on a tin roof. As Prunes watches the beans follow the flow of gravity, the manager's shadow blots out the twenty-watt bulb barely lighting the stairs.

"You're fired", Roars his tormentor.

In the darkness Prunes smiles.

Once again Prunes joins Red on the outside looking in. Of course, like Red's expulsion from the A&P he's barred permanently from the New York Store. Switching stores wasn't any problem for The Boys – the New York Store for Red and the A&P for Prunes - and like Red Prunes does his bit to ensure that the storeowners never forget their poor mother who was wasting away at home while The Boys did the weekly shopping.

Extortion is a nasty word. Artful persuasion is much nicer, and fits The Boys to a tee. Neither threats nor curses have any effect on them. They meet the merchants eye to eye, arguing prices, giving them the old soft shoe, getting their way. Ma calls it perseverance. The merchants call it something else.

Well sir, Red's enthusiasm for speed was undiminished. Bikes today, trains tomorrow, cars whenever. And the airplane is skirting his horizon. The flying machine is the stuff of imagination. Barnstormers put on their flights of daring do at the local airport, flying upside down, screaming dives with smoke billowing from the tails, walking on wings, passing from one plane to another without benefit of parachute. And afterwards, the pilots take payloads of wallet filled saps up to the clouds giving the locals a taste of adventure. Red has seen all this and his eyes glisten with anticipation.

A couple of houses down from Ma lived a smashing looking skirt that had a thing going with an honest to goodness pilot. Wearing a white scarf, the airman would show up in his sports roadster and give The Kid and his buddies a few words about the fine points of flying loops while Miss Wonderful, tapping her foot, darted thin smiles at the busters, praying they would disappear into the atmosphere.

Her hero made it a habit to roar over the neighborhood

waggling his wings smack dab over his intended's house regular as clockwork. Miss Wonderful's parents weren't too thrilled with lover boy strafing the neighborhood, but The Kid watched in awe. So did Red.

One bright summer day the love birds tied the knot and flew off into the sunset, Mr. Pilot and Mrs. Co-pilot barnstorming their way to everlasting happiness. The barnstormer was a great loss to The Kid, but he never suspected how much a loss he was to Red.

Even though the neighborhood quieted down a bit, the sight of that old biplane buzzing the housetops had captured the fertile brains of Red and his buddy Swede. With envious orbs they watched the lovesick barnstormer fly smack dab into the heart of the neighborhood doll. Adventure in the ozone was etched deeply into their psyches.

Red and his buddy Swede decide to give the airline industry their undivided attention, and for once they would carry out their plans legally. Which was no small decision as acting within the law went against everything they held dear.

They save up enough scratch for a one-way flight to Chicago - ten smackaroos - that is big bucks no matter how you cut it. Dressed in their Sunday best, they sit in the airport waiting room anticipating the flight, trying to act nonchalant. The plane takes off at ten, the skies clear, their adventure begins.

They're mighty impressed with the entire performance just a flying along listening to the engine roar and watching all those pitiful ant-like creatures chained to the ground. Here, soaring above the clouds, Red finds his destiny. Swede ain't too sure. With the plane bouncing around, his thoughts turn disturbingly to the pilot's competence.

The two warriors of the heavens are a brick shy when it comes to sophistication in the ways of modern air travel. So when the stewardess brings out a spot of lunch they accept with some trepidation. They ain't about to refuse the food, no sir, but having never been offered a free meal before, they are under the impression they had to pay for it. This should not have presented a problem but as they had dropped their entire fortunes buying their tickets, their pockets were, sad to say, empty.

Not to worry. Red sizes up the situation. The stewardess doesn't look too fast - running wise, that is - and he figures a quick sprint after they land will beat any meal check dropped on them. The two saps are so geared up that the plane door's hardly open when they bust down the tarmac and through the terminal, laughing all the way, telling each other how smart they had been. A meal without paying for it! What a blast.

They were in good old Chi in their Sunday best, taking in the city without a cent to their names. Neither of the darbs had given it much thought about getting back home so they assess their options, and with Red's vast experience ducking railroad coppers, elect to ride the rails. They wander around for hours, but finally find the switching yard and hop a freight headed west.

By this time their enthusiasm thins out, and the prospect of hanging on a filthy freight hauling coal darkens their outlook. For interminable hours in dropping temperatures they cling to the freight. The only things white between them were their knuckles. As the freight slows down passing through the East End two figures drop off, separating without words, sneaking home.

When Red slinks in - it is early in the a.m. - Ma spies what used to be her handsome son and nearly falls out of bed. His clothes blackened with soot, his shoes dulled beyond repair, his flashing smile a frozen grin, eyes mere slits filled with cinders, Red stands before her a pitiful mess.

But he explains the thrill of flying and how he has decided to become a pilot and how Ma'll be peacock proud of him when he makes his mark in the aviation business. Ma says he ought to take a good look at himself as she is wondering how in the world he escaped the crash without bodily injury.

Red's mind is going at a hundred per thinking up some plausible story that will explain how he gets back home, transportation wise, that is. He knows Ma is dead set against hopping freights, but since Ma seems to think his appearance stems from an airplane crash he decides to forget that part of his adventure. So he slides past the return trip from Chi as if it had never happened, and with Ma shaking her head and wondering out loud what will ever become of him, Red slips upstairs to bed.

The next day Red thrills The Kid with his flight to Chicago and the kinship he feels with the Wright brothers, and all. So how was the ride home, The Kid asks. Red swears The Kid to secrecy and whispers out the story of riding home between two coal cars.

Seems to me, The Kid says, that anybody with half a load would have figured out a way home before he left. Red glares at The Kid, tells him that when he grows up he'll understand, walks off with a disgusted look as if he had been wasting his time bringing the world of adventure to a punk kid.

It's about this time that Red drives into the back yard with a Model A which tick-tocks like Ma's alarm clock, and which, he claims, Russ down at the gas station sold him for a song. What the tune is Ma has no way of knowing, but she suspects some bohunk who wandered into one of Russ's after hours poker games lost his wheels to an inside straight which is too bad for the bohunk but okay for Red.

She hadn't tumbled to the fact that the Model A is costing Red bucks that are absent from his wallet, and in order to keep Jemima running he needs cash up front. He decides that too much book learning is destroying his fine-tuning, and school is a drag no matter how you cut it. Red's new motto is: "Work is in, school is out."

Red applies for a boy laborer job at the Rock Island Arsenal, and being wise beyond his years takes Prunes along the day he is scheduled to take the written exam. With Prunes cooling his heels outside the test room Red takes a gander at the math section and knows right away he is in deep trouble. Faking an urge he cannot control, he asked the examiner to be excused to go to the restroom. Exiting the room with the exam papers in his hand, he shoves them into Prunes' mitts, orders him to get inspired, and hurries off to the head

With Red sweating out his immediate future in the restroom Prunes whizzes through the math questions. Thumbs up nods Prunes and Red marches back to the test room. Faking his relief, he drops a mile wide grin on the examiner. He was only sixteen but as he told The Kid age is just a figure. The important thing was he got the job.

The straight of it is that Red when departs home each a.m. he's dressed just like he was going to high school. After breakfast, Red slips off each morning with a book under his arm that should have alerted Ma that what she is seeing is not what she's getting. Red is good at effects. With the book as a fooler he figures Ma'll never cotton to his flimflam.

Wrong. Even Ma can't help but notice he waltzes off with the same old book every day.

Now Ma is a firm believer in the educational process, never ever considers that one of her brood won't graduate from high school. When she discovers Red giving her the old two-step about skipping high school she about goes through the ceiling.

With her vocal cords extended like those of a Sergeant Major, she bellows, "What do you mean you quit school?"

Red puts his arm around her and says how much he loves her. All that sweet talk Ma is a sucker for. Besides - and here's where Red puts in the clincher - a few more green ones in the family treasury will surely help out. Ma's shoulders slump and she wipes away a tear or two, finally caves in, but not before she wonders out loud what will become of Red. With the depression never letting up and now Red dodging school her world is crashing down around her.

Fall slips into winter just like it is supposed to and everything seems to be clicking on all fours. Sis is bringing in the George Washingtons and Red is working and Ma is looking forward to a Christmas that for the first time in years would be truly bright. The snow comes right on time that makes for great sliding and skiing and The Kid yelps for joy.

Prunes is ready to assault the world's ski jump record and Red is egging him on which The Kid considers a right brotherly thing to do. Prunes shows off the skis he had repossessed from a trash pile and repaired last summer. Which was the time, you know, he had hacked Red's new bicycle tire in half. Prunes conveniently forgets about Red chasing him around the house, axe in hand threatening to decapitate him. No sir, no bad memories were gonna upset Prunes on his run to glory.

Prunes boasts about how cleverly he had screwed the curved front ends together, and now that the snow was packed down he was all set to make a run on the record.

Red listens to Prunes brag about how cleverly he had screwed the curved front ends together, and now that the snow was packed down he was all set to make a run at he record. But inside he is quivering with the knowledge that the only screws remaining in the skis are the ones in Prunes' imagination.

It's a tad unusual for Red to cheer Prune's endeavors, but as Christmas is nearby The Kid discards the red head's enthusiasm without a second thought. The East End Gang are all waiting for Prune's jump to victory, so whether Red is sincere or not is lost in the promise that for Prunes, his day had finally arrived.

One nicely lit Saturday after another snowfall, Prunes announces that this is the day. The Kid and his buddies troop up to a fair sized hill on the backside of the bluff to watch the event of the winter. Red is so enthused he lines up all the Neanderthals and The Kid's whizzers to build a right big ski jump near the bottom of the hill. The Kid had never seen Red so energetic about work, but crossed it off to the Christmas spirit.

Prunes trudges up to the top of the hill and when he has his shoes tucked snugly into the straps he waves down to the assembled bodies. Red signals back, giving out with a rousing cheer and Prunes takes off. With his skis polished to a fine hone, bees wax and all, down Prunes hurdles. It was the fastest ski run The Kid had ever witnessed.

When Prunes hits the jump the front ends of the skis explode and suddenly Prunes and his skis part company. Prunes heads east, the skis fly north and south. His screech echoing through out the bluff is terrible to hear. Openmouthed, The Kid claps his mittens over his ears, and when Prunes hits the snow-packed ground it is as if a sack of cement had been dropped from a five-story building. The Kid had never before heard such a sickening thud.

Everybody rushes over to Prunes lying flat on his back in a heap of snow. Asking nobody in particular, he croaks, "What went wrong - what went wrong?" Kinda weak-like. It was pathetic.

When he recovers, Prunes inspects the skis and finding no screws, had everybody searching the area. Red observes that the screws were probably buried in the snow, and when the snow melts in the spring Prunes will most likely find them all over the place. Red has a devil's grin on his puss that alerts The Kid that something is amiss. This accident, The Kid concludes, ain't no accident. The Kid pops Red the evil eye, deciding there is something going on of which he knows nothing about. Red winks back, but says nothing. Shazam, he hates mysteries.

That night lying in bed he hears Prunes mumbling about how he can't understand why the ends of his skis disintegrated so easily when he's absolutely positive he had screwed them tight. Asks Red if he had any ideas on the subject.

Red applies a half-hitch to the laugh that's lurking in his chest, replies that in all seriousness it is beyond him,

"Screws should have held, no question about that," Red says.

Silence.

In the dark The Kid could almost *feel* Red's grin, and remembering his brother's wink up by the sky jump, he decided sooner or later he'd get the right of it.

As for Red, revenge had never been sweeter.

In the fruit room, just off the basement stairs, Ma's summer treasures were set lovingly on shelves. Mason jars filled with tomatoes, beans and other garden vegetables were lined up like obedient soldiers. A few store bought can goods, pork and beans mainly, sat alongside, but if it were not for Ma's jars of garden produce her brood would have starved in the long winter months. Ma knew to the last jar how much she had laid aside on the fruit room shelves. She should have been a cabinet member for President Roosevelt in charge of the economy or budget.

Anyway, when the yule season stuck its nose in the door Ma anticipated one of the jobs she really enjoyed. Tucked behind the shiny jars of beans sat Ma's bottle of brandy that she used in her fruitcake recipe. According to the neighbors, Ma did a right smart job on her fruitcakes. And her secret, of course, was a touch or two of brandy that made the cakes awfully presentable.

One snowy day The Kid trips down to the cellar and finds Red measuring the level of Ma's brandy bottle. Intent on Red's line of sight and a glass of water in his hand, Prunes' attention is riveted on the brandy bottle. The conspirators neither see nor hear him.

"What cha doing?" The Kid asks innocently.

The Boys almost leap out of their skins. About drop the brandy bottle, too. Next thing The Kid knows, he is thrust up against the wall listening to threats which, to put it kindly, meant that if he so much as *breathed* a word The Boys'd pulverize puny frame. Since Prunes and Red have him by age, weight, height and smarts, The Kid takes the threats right seriously, deciding that life's wondrous adventures might be slipping away from him if he didn't promise to shut his worthless trap. The Kid raises his hand like he's giving a right serious Boy Scout oath. Promises his everlasting silence. That he had been fired from the Scouts was best not talked about.

So he quick steps out of the fruit cellar wondering all the while about what his brothers were doing with the brandy bottle. Like a festering sore, he can't keep his thinker off it. Occasionally - well more like every other day - he checks the bottle, but the brandy remains at the same level. After giving the problem his best Sherlock Holmes deductive process, The Kid finally tumbles to The Boys action. Prunes and Red were taking a nip or two now and then from Ma's Christmas spirits, then filling the bottle back up to its original level with some of the Mississippi's best H2O. Of course, the brandy's getting weaker and weaker, but numb and dumb figure Ma will never catch them.

Just before Christmas Ma proceeds to make all her famous fruit cakes with the traditional splash of brandy to give it that smacky good taste. But when she taste tests one of the cakes she knows immediately she'd been flimflammed. No zing in the fruitcakes meant no brandy in the bottle. Ma is, as they say, fit to be tied. She gives The Kid a piece and asks him for an opinion.

Normally The Kid would throw up his hands and tell her what a grand job she has done, but like good old George, he cannot tell a lie. Well, not much of one anyway. The Kid licks his lips and gives out with a far off stare, says with all due deliberation the cake's got a sawdust taste.

"Gosh darn it," he says with a straight face, "I wonder why?"

Ma sets her chin, glares at The Kid with her this-calls-for-an-inquisition face, and disgustedly puts the cakes aside for the visiting hobos. The Kid skedaddles.

That evening the brood is sitting at the kitchen table working over one of Ma's cream this or that on toast. The Kid senses that Ma is working up to something special because she is a mite quiet during the meal, not asking questions or anything. Sis, Ma's eldest and also smartest, is Ma's confidant which, The Kid decides, had something to do with her being a girl and all that. But if you knew, really knew, Ma don't have much of a choice. Even if Prunes or Red had been the eldest, Ma would have selected Sis. Sis had responsibility written all over her, and unlike The Boys, still had the brains God had given her. Ma is thankful for that.

So Ma returns to normal and asks Sis sweetly, "By the way, do you know what happened to the brandy I had hidden in the fruit room?" Sis puckers her brow, says something like whatever do you mean, Ma?

The Kid is enjoying the by-play, knows instinctively that the game, as Sherlock declared, is afoot.

Ma turns to Buddy and Jacky who are all of a sudden not swallowing too good. "Boys, what happened to the brandy?" With her tone just this side of a twenty to life sentence, Ma directs the question with force, just like Mr. District Attorney her favorite radio star.

The Kid wonders how the East End sharks are going to swim free of her net. Both of the wonders mumble that they haven't the slightest what Ma is talking about. But their eyes deceive them. Looking down and kinda shifty-like. Watching Ma reel in the culprits, The Kid decides he is getting a first class lesson.

Ma pursues the criminals responsible for her weak-kneed brandy like J. Edgar Hoover tracking down John Dillinger. She has them cornered, but the wisenheimers refuse to crack. She goes on and on about how embarrassed she is that the old fruit cakes taste like so much sawdust, and that she can't even give the crummy messes away, and what with the neighbors expecting her tasty Christmas gift, what is she to do? The Kid allows as to how Ma might consider using his Dick Tracy fingerprint kit on the brandy bottle and she will have the offenders dead to rights.

Shooting big time lasers at The Boys, Ma says to The Kid that she knows exactly who has been tampering with her brandy and if there isn't some confessing done pretty soon there will be two less plates at the table. This is serious because The Boys are in that eating stage which requires a zillion calories a day just to keep them from death's door.

But the co-conspirators sit there stonewalling which upsets Ma no end because when she expects a confession SHE EXPECTS A CONFESSION. Every so often as Ma is running down, Prunes and/or Red shoot threatening glances at The Kid as if to say, "Keep your stupid mouth shut - or else."

The Kid ain't about to get into that or else business, so he sits quietly watching the criminal justice system in action. He has to give his brothers credit. Sweat pours down their miserable pusses, but they won't admit to a thing.

After a silence which seems to last a couple of hours, Ma and Sis jump up and clear the table. The Kid stares at The Boys and, glassy-eyed they stare back. Like whipped puppies, they are guilty as charged, but by golly, they hadn't confessed.

Well, Ma makes a whole new batch of fruitcakes that according to the neighbors are about the best they had ever tasted. Which means there is a new brandy bottle stashed someplace in the old homestead. One day The Kid bumps into Red searching the fruit room, knows the old red head won't be satisfied until he finds the brandy. For Red, it's a matter of honor.

THE WITCHING HOUR

Bob and Swede Johnson

On the evening Martians were supposedly invading New York we were up on the bluff, plotting and planning our raids, bent on harassing the neighborhood. Must have had every kid in the East End up there.

It was, you see, Halloween . . .

The Kid was a bit older now, no longer a whizzer wearing short pants but not grown up either. To him, the East End remained the same, a succulent oyster ripe for the shucking. Each day held the promise of adventure, and when The Kid woke up he hit the deck with his eyes wide open. He didn't cotton to the idea that he had to grow up, "to understand." If he had heard those words once he had heard them a zillion times from Ma and Sis and Prunes and Red. Cripes, even from Russ. Adventure was lying outside the back door, sneaky-like, waiting just for him.

"Did ya hear about Blackie Cole's dog?"

Russ was busy pulling a nail the size of a broom handle from old man Siegers beat up Model A. Usually Russ whistled when he worked, but now he tugged and sweated and swore. The tire was bald and thin as tissue paper and for the umpteenth time Russ had failed to sell the old man a new one.

"Fix 'er up best ya can," ordered old Sieger.

The Kid listens to Russ make his all-American sales pitch, but as usual gets nowhere with the sodbuster. The Kid figures Russ'll perk up when he hears about the latest episode involving Blackie Cole and the Young Turks who slurped up all Blackie's home distilled booze. The Kid ain't about to allow Russ's foul mood to interrupt his story so he plows right along.

Seems Blackie and the Young Turks been slugging it down all day, and they're having a merry time hooting and hollering and chasing one another all over the bluff. About dark the boozers line up on Blackie's front porch talking nonsense and watching the world go by when this dog starts a yowling and won't quit. Blackie, who by this time can't even recognize it's his own dog's yapping, grabs his rifle waving it all over the place trying to get a bead on the offending cur. One of the Turks snatches the rifle from Blackie and disposes of the offending cur with one shot which, for the moment, makes Blackie one happy rum runner.

Blackie staggers over to the critter and gives out with a painful yelp. Finds his favorite dog deader 'an a doornail. The old boozer swears something awful - you could hear him all over the neighborhood - then recovering his rifle, he starts blasting away in the general direction of the Turks. The nitwits are bailing out in all directions, taking cover in the woods or sliding down the bluff. Blackie is hell bent after his best customers, firing away, hitting mostly trees of which there are quite a few.

Finally, answering the neighborhood tom-toms, the coppers zoom up, and after putting the arm on Blackie they confiscate all his illegal booze. Which must have been considerable because they require a truck to haul the stuff away.

"Pretty darned exciting, don't ya think?"

Russ has the tire back on old Sieger's Model A deciding he'll charge Sieger four bits which will probably bring on a heart attack, but he's sick and tired of arguing with the old man who the wiseguys claim has a couple thousand smackeroos buried behind the out house.

Russ grunts, "Yeah, kid, exciting."

The Kid follows Russ into his office, sits when Russ sits. The morning was cool and crisp, and the leaves were showing their fall colors, a time for thinking, for doing nothing at all. The Kid slumps in an old beat up chair off in the corner wondering whether he ought to tell Russ about his latest predicament. Russ has his feet perched up on a crummy oak desk begrimed with spills of motor oil and grease, but otherwise quite grand for a business that catered to the whims of the tight-fisted motoring public. A pile of new tires stand near the door the odd smell of rubber wafting through the office.

Ever since he had found out the truth of the matter, The Kid had wanted to talk his problem over with Russ, figuring he needed some of Russ's expert advice. It was unfair, that's what it was, by golly. As he begins to think about the situation, a sober expression crosses The Kid's puss.

"I need some advice."

Russ peers over his brand new cheaters, asks not too enthusiastic, "What kind of advice?"

"Well, I got this problem with Prunes and Red."

Russ sits back polishing his cheaters as if he's interested, so The Kid takes this as a go ahead, remembers not to mumble because this is a sure fire way to lose Russ.

Prunes and Red and The Kid sleep in the attic. Each has a bed that fits in cubicle called a dormer. In the summer the attic's insufferably hot and in the winter their breath freezes solid on their pillows. Undressing over the hot air register in the kitchen, The Kid dons his flannel pajamas and dashes to the attic carrying a hot water bottle to warm the sheets. Ma had the strange belief that fresh air made for a healthy body, hence the small dormer windows were open regardless of the temperature. The Kid had long ago decided that even the North Pole couldn't be colder, but what Ma said went.

Prunes and Red, don't ya know, were of an age to stay out late. On the weekends they prowl around the rural towns, going to dances and eyeing the dolls. By the time The Boys hit the attic The Kid had preceded them to the Antarctic by a few time zones and was fast asleep. Seeing their little brother in a warm toasty bed dreaming half his life away, Prunes and Red lift him up gently and deposit him in one of the cold beds. Then they jump in The Kids comfy spot and snooze the night away.

It was a long time before The Kid figures out why he was waking up in a different bed all scrunched up, shivering like Blackie Cole's once was dog. The Boys tell him that he was probably sleep walking and promise to keep an eye on him in case he wanders too far from home.

"Can you beat it," says The Kid. "I believed the busters. But then it gets to me that the only time I wake up in another bed is during the winter."

Russ is starting to fade fast so The Kid hurries up.

By the time he cottons onto his brother's treachery it is spring, but he swears he'd get a payback. Now as he sits in Russ's office, he decides good old Russ'd set him straight.

Eyes covered with the *Moline Daily Dispatch* and sounding like a fast freight highballing through the East End, Russ snores away. Shucks, no telling when Russ'll come to. The Kid scrunches down in his chair, and joins Russ in dreamland . . . .

The Kid lay there all shrunk up in the cold bed, no sign of life. Ma is dabbing at her eyes and Doc Bones pulls the listening device off his ears.

"Madam, he's a gonner. Just shriveled to death, body temperature ought degrees. Medical science," the doc says, "has claimed another case of coldbeditis." The good doc sighs, "There is no cure. I'd better call the meat wagon."

Ma passes a pitiful look at The Kid's inert body then raises her arm and points to The Boys slinking down in the corner of the dormer. "There they are officer. The rascals did this to my darling boy, one cold bed too many. He never had a chance. And to think he would have been one of the best third baseman the Cubs ever had."

Tall as ever in his greatcoat, Officer Larson yells, "Finally. I've been after these two twisters for the past five years and now I've got them red handed. Ha,Ha,Ha. Don't worry one bit Madam, they'll be tossed in the slammer for life, in the darkest hole of Calcutta to be fed on bread and water till the end of time, or the end of their worthless lives, whichever come first. . . . . .

With a smile on his puss The Kid comes out of his reverie. He glances across at Russ who wakes himself up with an enormous snort that blows the newspaper clean off his face and across the room.

Russ clears his brain cells. "Something you were saying kid?"

"Nope." The Kid concludes that come winter he'll have a surprise for Prunes and Red. Just what kind of bombshell remains to be planned, maybe a couple of dead garter snakes in their pillows or what about tossing a firecracker in their beds? Yeah, he would figure out something. No need to bother Russ with the details.

Russ stretches and yawns, focusing his eyes on the local news. From the local daily rag dangling in his hands Russ reads out loud that the mayor promised to crack down unmercifully on Halloween pranksters. The Kid's ears pick up.

About this time each year the adult population gathered together to exchange tidbits about the escalating harassment they had to endure at Halloween. One and all were mighty sick and tired of all this foolishness, and they enjoined the city fathers into action - with a capital A - to root out these unhealthy inclinations on the part of a select group of local hoodlums who, thank heavens, were not their own beloved offspring.

Russ laughs, tells The Kid it is exactly their offspring who committed these awful crimes against humanity. He passes the paper across to The Kid, and there belly to the west wind, stands Fred Hines pointing to a farm wagon that is sitting all proud-like on top of his barn. The picture is a repeat from last year.

The Kid remembers it well, eyes Russ and tells him what's what. In a weak moment Prunes and Red give The Kid their account of the incident that The Kid ought to know, by now skirts the truth by a zillion miles or so. Red claims that a bunch of highbinders from across the river worked all night disassembling old Fred's wagon, then reconstructed it on the peak of his barn. With straight faces, Prunes and Red praise these unknown conspirators for their inspired engineering feat, but The Kid believed that like he'd believed the tooth fairy.

To believe some, "gang of foreigners," had pulled off this prank in the East End was ridiculous. Nothing moved in or out of the East End without Prunes or Red or the lunkheads they ran with from knowing about it, so The Kid cottoned to the fact that the Neanderthals had been hard at work last Halloween. Besides, it was the same wagon Prunes had refurbished for The Kid's greatest ride of his life.

Problem was, the dummies hadn't figured out that Fred Hines harvested up all this notoriety like a movie star signing autographs for the local yokels. With his photo splashed all over the front page and giving interviews to all the local scribes, Fred smiled and joked about how much he had grown used to that darned old wagon sitting atop his barn. Gave the farm a bit of class, by golly.

"Tell 'em to come back next year and take 'er down," Fred tells the press. Fat chance that would occur, but it did set The Kid to thinking.

Russ says The Kid is right as rain, but he better keep his fanny in doors this Halloween because this copper friend of his says they were going to be out in force ready to put the arm on any smart aleck stupid enough to test the law. The Kid gives Russ a you-must-be-kidding look and saunters on home.

On Halloween eve The Kid, Davey and Johnny are laying down under the old oak tree waiting for the troops to gather, discussing what to do and who to do it to. As the stand-up guys from the far reaches of the East End arrive, The Kid waits for some grand plan to emerge, but he obtains nothing original. New ideas were harder to come by than a pocket full of loose change.

Duffy allows as to how the old garbage can trick is a gooder. Tying a rope the width of 5th avenue to two garbage cans and hiding in the bushes with the rope laying flat on the avenue is a sure fire success when some unsuspecting motorist comes chugging along and hears the garbage cans clattering and banging behind him. Pulling the rope taut at the right time requires a deft touch, Duffy declares.

The Kid's getting more disgusted by the minute. Cripes, the garbage can trick is so old that the victims ain't swearing and carrying on anymore, so what's the use? If he's going to top Prunes and Red, he needs a grabber.

One of the mentally deficient proposes that the old paper bag filled with crapola from Fred Hines farmyard was just the ticket. Davey gives the buster a where-did-you-come-from sneer, but Hooter claims it takes courage to sneak up to some bohunk's front porch, setting the bag of crapola on fire and ringing the doorbell.

And who, The Kid asks disgustedly, is still left in the neighborhood dumb enough to charge out and stamp out the fire? Who?

"Old lady Reece," declares a voice in the dark.

"You must be off your rocker," comes another voice.

Silence.

Maybe asking for new ideas from this bunch of losers is more than The Kid can expect. Here they sit in the dark on the biggest night of the year and they're blathering about pulling the same old tricks over and over. Somebody ought to have a revelation.

It seemed a shame the dunces were so blank what with Satan right out there throwing around one terrific prank after another in the breeze. All Lucifer needed was a solid bunch of upright guys to grab ahold of his inspiration and carry out his devilment. The Kid had spread the word that this was going to be a Halloween to end all Halloweens, but at the moment the prospect seemed mighty dim.

A couple of backbenchers work the garbage can trick a few times, but The Kid and the inner circle watched disinterestedly from the bluff. The party was as flat as one of old man Sieger's bald tires when Billy Hastings wonders aloud whether Mr. Johnson's horses might be put to use.

Billy, a short pants punk who lived next door to The Kid, shouldn't have been roustin' around with the older guys but The Kid didn't have the heart to tell him to get lost. Besides, the little buster had just come up with a right smart idea.

"SHAZAM," yelps The Kid. Now to put 'er into action.

Mr. Johnson is a construction man of no small note, and he keeps those wooden frames called horses all stacked behind his garage. Billy says they are sitting there just for the taking so the gang whoops and hollers and give Billy a few right smart slaps on the back for bringing up this grand idea.

Ideas are one thing but carrying them out, now there's the

rub. The wiseacres gather around and a council of war lays out a battle plan. The Kid's ecstatic.

The All-American East End Team shoot down to Johnson's garage and heist a few wooden horses. Staggering the horses, first in one lane then the other about fifty feet apart on the avenue under the bluff, the revelers create a drivers obstacle course. On-coming cars ain't completely blocked off, but it takes a steady hand to dodge through the blockade.

Listening to the swearing and threats of bodily harm float up from the avenue, the pranksters on the bluff watch the drivers wind their cars around the blockade then speed off. Which is a bit of okay, but not good enough. Hooter says why not block the oldsters in completely. The Kid shrugs and says yeah, why not? So when the next car slams to a screeching stop before a completely blocked avenue, the merry band hear a bit of real first class cussing.

Raising his fist to the bluff, the driver gets out and tosses the horses on the boulevard, all the while blueing up the horizon with some choice obscenities. Overcome with delight, the misfits roll around on the ground, slapping each other on the back and generally having a high old time.

Then Dink's mother gets caught in the net. Her eye hand coordination, like the Dinks, went west with the gold rush. Bottle bottom glasses to boot. Anyway, Dink's mother crashes into one of the horses and she emerges from the driver's seat confused no end. This sets up a stadium-like cheer from the bluff which courses through the trees and echoes down the avenue. Dink's mother scans her eyes upwards, and although she can't see worth a darn she knows who the busters are. One and all.

The question passes through The Kid's thinker why Dink ain't present, but figures Dink's mother has him trussed up in the basement to keep him safe from the devil's playground. Gee whillikers, all this fun and the Dink's missing out on it. Too bad.

The Kid watches her car drive off and begins laying bigger and better plans.

With this success, all the merry makers want to get in on the act so a search party sneaks out to gather every wood horse that could be found in the East End. The Kid sets up a command post on the bluff, right under the old oak tree, and from there directs the streets and alleys to be blockaded. As irate motorists remove a blockade a team of pranksters sneak back in and reset the horses. Then the coppers showed up.

Some squealer has reported a serious traffic hazard on 5th avenue, and the squad cars come roaring in, spotlights spraying the alleys and bluff. One of the squad cars with its lights off rolls silently up the alley, but Hooter and H from the back, and The Kid and Johnny from the front, block the coppers in which raises the temperature of the boys in blue no little.

Back up on the bluff some of the steam was running out of the lesser fun-makers. Fooling around with the public was one thing, but taking on the coppers raised the ante a mite steep.

The fair weather busters are taking a hike for home, but Davey spots another squad car skulking up the alley. "These guys are mine," he yelps.

Off to do battle go Davey and Duffy and Hooter and the H, and quickly another squad car is blockaded. Suddenly, uniforms are charging all over the neighborhood that is a signal for retreat. Hooter zigzags it between houses with a copper grunting right behind him. Unable to shake the blue coat, Hooter heads for the creek and with a mighty leap clears it. The copper is about ten feet short.

Now the neighborhood is filled with some first class swearing. Police radios blaring out identifications: "Get the sucker in the red sweatshirt . . . Spotted a twirp wearing a blue baseball cap . . Jeez, Marty fell in the creek . . Where did all these whizzers come from . . ."

Some of Red's sage advice comes back to The Kid: "If some copper's hot after your body, get home quick, change clothes and grab a book. Then when the law comes to the door accusing you of some crime against humanity, Ma'll demand a positive identification and ten to one the blue coats will take a look at you and be unsure since you are dressed differently and looking studious as all get out."

So following his deserting troops, The Kid skedaddles home and is just about in the door when he remembers Billy Hastings. Hadn't seen the little shaver since the coppers put in an appearance. Peering into the darkness, The Kid decides it is clear of blue coats. He slinks quietly over to the Hastings back door, but just then he spots a flashlight from the far corner of the Hastings garage. As H was the only guy who had a flashlight, The Kid sneaks over to the light and whispers, "Douse the light, H. Coppers are all over the place."

The hand that grabbed him wasn't on the end of H's arm.

Tossed into the back seat of the squad car, The Kid finds Mickey the Mope scrunched up against the far corner. Now Mickey lived a far piece away, but as he later explained, he just couldn't miss out on all the fun. Said he was walking down the main drag when the coppers put the grab on him. Despite his pleas of innocence, the uniforms warn him to shut up. Then, they toss him in the squad car where The Kid finds him feeling mighty low.

The Kid figures the coppers are going to give them an old fashion lecture about endangering life and property and let them go, but such was not to be. Mickey and The Kid sit in the squad car listening to the chases, the curses, the, "got cha's." Before long the neighborhood dust up is down to zero. The Kid eyes Ma's back door and thoughts of flight to another country cross his mind. Jeez, he hopes Billy Hastings is safe in bed.

It's embarrassing and no less scary. The Kid can't figure out what the big deal is all about. The Hooter and Duffy and Mickey the Mope and The Kid are standing before the local magistrate listening to the coppers inform the judge about these, "hundreds," of wayward boys who attempted to take over the East End. The officers maintain they had received zillions of phone calls from irate citizens complaining that if the police can't get the situation under control they better turn in their blues because they'd all be looking for jobs in the a.m.

One slightly wet and muddy copper testifies how he had this speedster in the red sweatshirt in his grasp but missed jumping the creek by a foot or two, and now has this severe back sprain and probably will have to go to the hospital. The copper warms up to his subject telling the judge that he had to listen to the wisenhimer laugh at him as he slowly sank to the bottom of the creek. The judge tosses Hooter the fish eye. It just so happens Hooter is wearing a red sweatshirt.

So the magistrate sits there listening to all these tales of woe, and how much danger these four half-grown busters are to the community, and what is the world coming to when decent citizens can't drive the East End streets without risking life and limb.

The Kid believes they were simply engaged in a little Halloween sport, not a threat to mankind. Occasionally, he wonders about what went wrong, but the court room scene is too much for a half-grown buster who has a session with another judge sitting at home, and that judge he don't want to think about.

Finally, the magistrate has enough doom and gloom. He releases the hard-bitten criminals and sets sentencing for the next week. It is a cruel, cruel world.

Ma looks at The Kid as if he had betrayed her, God and country. She tells Sis that The Kid will never ever be able to obtain a decent job what with a criminal record and all the notoriety. The Kid hangs his head, figures he's really done it this time. The family name is damaged beyond repair.

The *Dispatch* runs an article naming names about how the police stymied a plot against the residents of the East End and how brave the coppers were in responding to this serious societal problem. The mayor takes credit for managing the crisis that sounds a heck of a lot more serious than the pranks of four snot-nosed kids. Then again, the snot-nosed kids don't have much to say about what the mayor thinks about the incident.

Next week, hair slicked down and shoes polished The Kid, Duffy, Hooter and Mickey appear before the magistrate, innocent babes ready to throw themselves on the mercy of the court. Didn't work. With a stern face the judge hands down a $25.00 fine to each of the wastrels for actions detrimental to the stability of the community.

When the amount of the fine gets through to his foggy brain cells, The Kid nearly faints. None of the pranksters had twenty-five cents let alone 25 George Washingtons. Then a look of compassion crosses the judge's puss, and he decrees the fines would be paid through community service. The Kid sighs, thankful as all get out because he figures he was jailbait for sure. Washing squad cars at a dollar a car wasn't too bad come to think of it. Might even be through by Christmas.

Davey follows this criminal case of the century with a great deal of attention, tells The Kid there are no less than a zillion guys who beat the rap because their feet were faster than The Kid's. But putting that aside, he'd like to help out. Being a fair-minded, stand up guy Davey offers to wash a few squad cars. "What the hey, we're buddies ain't we?"

The Kid takes this as a capital idea, so Davey washes more than a few pounds of dirt from the squad cars. But his good deed doesn't last long. One Saturday when Davey is signing The Kid's name to the work sheet the duty sergeant warns him that if he ever sees his worthless hide in the police garage again he'll haul him straight away to Statesville, a prison well known for holding top mobsters and the like.

Davey grabs The Kid in school and whispers that he won't be laundering any more cars for him. Which upsets The Kid no end. He figures he is on the fast track to the big house, a hardened criminal before his time.

When The Kid appears at the police garage he's ready to hand in his, "Go Directly To Jail," card, but the Sergeant grunts that he has had enough of The Kid and his traveling band of wiseacres. He orders The Kid to clear out and never show his face again.

The Kid makes tracks.

The next day Davey sidles up to The Kid and swears him to secrecy. Davey claims that it was Dink's mother who had called the coppers on them. "Don't you remember that it was her car that hit one of the barricades?"

The Kid allows as to how he was so busy directing traffic that night he hadn't the time to recall every darned event that happened, and besides how does Davey know Dink's mother squealed?

Davey says that she had about chained Dink to a chair when she went out on Halloween eve, so when she returns home she *knows* Dink ain't been with the gang of malcontents. So, she's perfectly free to call the coppers knowing that her precious Dink is at home trussed up safe and sound. Davey's reasoning sounds okay, but The Kid asks why Davey is so sure somebody else didn't call in the alarm?

"Think about it. With the entire school population out on the streets, do you imagine any parent is going to call the coppers on one of his own?" Davey smirks, says there are times when he has real doubts about The Kid's ability to wade through adult thinking.

The Kid agrees, but he still harbors a grudge against the blue coats. He figures the right thing they could done was just given them a right serious tongue lashing and forgotten all about the arresting business.

The Halloween prank might have gotten more play school, but the teachers were all breathless talking about the radio show,

War Of The Worlds. It seemed the entire east coast evacuated when they listened to reports that Martians had invaded some one-horse town called Grovers Mills in New Jersey. The grown-ups never cottoned to the fact that it was only a science fiction radio show. The papers showed farmers in their pickups with shotguns aimed at the sky ready to blast the non-existent Martians.

The Kid thinks it's pretty funny, but Prunes says it weren't only the sodbusters on the east coast who were frightened to death. Prunes claims they found old lady Masterson sitting on top of her radio screaming like a banshee and it takes several white coats to cart her off to funny farms.

The Kid wishes he had heard the show, but all in all deems it a godsend. With the neighbors all excited over the Martian threat, and the state of old lady Masterson they consider the Halloween prank he and his buddies had engineered small time stuff indeed.

Once again he is slumped in Russ's old beat up chair, this time reviewing the entire matter of Halloween and the embarrassment he caused Ma. The Kid mentions that things are really grim on the old home front. Russ grunts, says The Kid must have a porous brain not to have figured out that he and his buddies had been sentenced as, "examples."

The Kid raises his orbs a smidgen, gives Russ that what-do-you-mean look.

"Look here Kid," Russ says, "the city fathers are filled up to their eyeballs with all the complaining about vandalism in the East End. They were out to nab Red and Prunes and the sharpies they run with, but when they grab you half-grown busters blocking the squad cars in the alley the uniforms figure a bird in the hand is worth two in the bush. Ha, Ha, Ha."

This puts a new perspective on The Kid's thinking. Wow, the coppers were really after Red and Prunes, but since they couldn't nail the Neanderthals they had put the screws to The

Kid and his cronies. Brother, a guy couldn't trust anybody these days. As The Kid departs, Russ produces a toothy grin.

Now all The Kid had to do is come up with an idea that will help Ma forget his brush with the men in blue.

Sitting in the front room he stares at his trumpet to which he had become and unwilling partner. Practice had become a pain in the nether reaches, even though, he had to admit, he wasn't too bad a tooter. Second trumpet in the school band that featured Louie Belson, son of the Music Man, on the drums. Now there was a real talent who was certain to be one of the premier jazz drummers in the country.

As he tootled his thinker got caught up in what he could do to get back into Ma's good graces. His brush with the men in blue still lingered in the old homestead, an aroma that predicted an uncertain future. That it was just possible that he wouldn't replace Stan Hack as the Cubs third baseman was enough to call into question his normal upbeat attitude that held his clouds were lined in silver. It was mighty cloudy these days but of silver there was no trace. He put his trumpet in its case and headed over to Chuck's store to pick up the *Dispatch* and fold the papers prior to walking his paper route.

Neither the hot summer days nor the cold winters stayed his chores. His paper route ran from 45th Street to 50th Street, from two houses atop the bluff to homes and shacks on the river road, including Mr. Erickson, the smokehouse man. Climbing up the bluff and scooting over the railroad tracks slick with snow or wet with rain tested his tenacity, but the thought of giving up never entered his mind. He passed up to eighty papers, and in a pinch passed the route up to 55th Street. Another sixty papers were a bit much, but he never complained. Once a yapper of a pooch bit him on the ankle and when Ma saw the blood she made tracks for the offending dog and its owner. The Kid heard but never saw that dog again.

On Saturdays he was up early collecting from sleepy customers, many who did not appreciate his enterprise. Then downtown to the Dispatch office where he turned in his weekly take listening to Mel chastising him for not collecting from the, "deadbeats." The slow pays were having a tough time so he listened to their excuses and let it go, sometimes week after week. After his session with Mel he spent the rest of the day being the office gofer, making an extra dollar. In good weeks he made over three dollars, a small fortune or so he thought.

Later when no longer a paperboy, he wrapped bundles for the men driving the rural routes, put up the baseball scores and Friday evening football games on a wire across the big window fronting the main drag. Holding a trainee driver's license he drove the International truck through the East End out to the East Moline State Hospital. An inmate named Pat would take the five papers and say, "Thank you, Oink, Oink." The Kid thought this was funny, but he muted his laughter until out of Pat's hearing.

One wintry night with the wind whistling through the trees and a full moon shadowing the landscape the International stalled just after he had given Pat his papers. Despite The Kids repeated attempts the truck wouldn't start so he hightailed it to the admin office.

"I'll get you," shrieked a voice from above. Looking up The Kid spies an old lady spread-eagled against the window bars. "I see you, I'll get you." Then high-pitched laughter screamed from her twisted mouth. Setting the dash record for panicked busters his feet may or may not have touched terra firma en route to the admin office. Shaking as if he had a major case of palsy, he called the Dispatch for assistance. Old Tom chuckled, "You probably flooded it. Get back in and hold the foot-feed down as you crank the starter.

"Yeah, but what if it still doesn't start."

"Keep trying."

"KEEP TRYING." Near panic, he heard himself whimper. *"She's crazy I tell you."*

"Ha, Ha, Ha," Click.

The Kid turned to the guard and in a quavering voice implored him to help him out – translation: *walk him past the loony to his paper truck.*

"Can't leave here," returned the guard.

"Yeah' but . ." stuttered The Kid, eyes bulging.

Screwing up what little courage he had left, The Kid again set a dash record taking in the loony's screams likening his body to that of a ripe cadaver. With shaking fingers he inserted the key and holding down the gas pedal per instructions:

THE DAMNED TRUCK STARTED!

It was the fastest exit from the East Moline State Hospital ever recorded.

And The Kid got back in Ma's good graces. During WWII he sold defense stamps. And got his photo in the Dispatch.

GRANDPA

1937 Visit: Aunt Belle, Bob, Helen, Mom, Jack & Grandpa

One fine summer day Ma gets a letter from out east saying that Grandpa is feeling poorly. Being a ninety plus senior Ma thinks the kiddos ought to see him before he passes into the great beyond. During a family meeting of the kitchen cabinet it is decided Red will drive them to New York to see Grandpa. Since The Kid has never before been out of the East End, he gets some maps from Russ and plans the route like a veteran tripper.

With Ma sitting proudly in the front seat and Sis and Prunes and The Kid in the back Red plunks along Route 6 at forty per, stopping every hour or so to check the oil level. Must have used a hundred quarts of Russ's Texaco on the trip. They stop along road side turnabouts to wolf down Ma's home baked bread and Prunes' stash of peanut butter, and apples and oranges. Stuff like that.

It is high adventure for The Kid. Sits on a stool forking down his breakfast in those glitzy railroad dining cars with neon signs flickering, "EATS, EATS, EATS," beds down in motor courts that have a gaggle of little cottages where, according to the notices at the desk, the sheets were changed every day. Up early they washed and brushed their teeth in cold water from the pump.

They played games and shouted out Burma Shave signs that kept the whole troop laughing.

"Hardly A Dream/Is Now Alive

Who Passed/On Hills/At Seventy-Five"

When they arrive in this one-horse hamlet in New York they find Grandpa spry and chipper as all get out. Stands up ramrod straight and claims he never felt better. This news brightens Ma no end as she had the idea he was headed directly for the bone yard. The brood line up in order and each say how wonderful it is to see him leaving out the word alive that he knows is on their minds but don't say.

Aunt Belle, a grim lipped old maid, is kinda sour grapes if ya asked The Kid. Anyway, to ensure Aunt Belle that The Kid was up to snuff with his religious duties Ma made him study the catechism on the trip out. Under Aunt Belle's penetrating orbs he dutifully recited, sometimes not, answers to her grilling. She informed Ma that the boy was lax, that he required further study. Ma wasn't too thrilled with the old maid's attitude, but she eyed The Kid who by this time had a case of the sweats. "See, I told you study harder."

Aunts and Uncles, all Irish Catholics to the core came to visit. They acted as if they were on an inspection tour. Except for Uncle Chester, he with the huge red mustache, they were not too lively. Their interests ran to farming, blathered about the weather and the crops, nothing important like baseball that consumed The Kids waking moments. Having never forgiven Will Glendon for marrying a Scots Presbyterian some referred to Ma as, "Mrs. Glendon," just as Sis once told him. Unlike the Munro Clan who kissed everybody in sight there was none of that kissing stuff in Honeoye Falls.

Grandpa bought him a hardball. He tossed it against the barn door, but with no return he got tired of fetching it. Grandpa should have bought him a rubber ball, but not knowing squat about baseball The Kid just shook his head. With no one to play catch with he returned to the front porch where Grandpa is going to and fro on his rocking chair listening to Ma and Sis. Grandpa says sit and he sits. Inspired The Kid asks if he had seen any Burma Shave signs. Receiving a nod, he recites:

"Within This Vale/ of Toil/ And Sin
Your Head/ Grows Bald/ But Not Your Chin"

Grandpa, who has his original hair although a mite gray, gives out with a laugh and says to Ma what a quick study The Kid is and since tomorrow is Sunday he'll drive to church which he hasn't done for a while.

Ma backs up a bit, says kinda loud into Grandpa's ear, "Alone I trust." Grandpa imparts a sly grin, tells Ma that it's time for the younger to hit the road with his only living grandfather and he won't take no for an answer.

A stricken look passes over Ma's face, but The Kid blurts out, "WOW!"

Grandpa takes The Kid out to the barn and there stands his funeral black Model T. Proudly shows him the varnish job he applies to it every year that accounts for its glistening finish. The Kid is mighty impressed, can hardly wait until the next day. He doesn't notice Sis staring up to the heavens nor the worried looks crossing the pusses of Prunes and Red.

On the appointed a.m., dressed in his Sunday best, The Kid

assists Grandpa into the Model T. Ma has a funny look, says real loud as if Grandpa's hearing had been shipped back to the old sod that she insists he drive carefully and that they'll meet at the church which is only a few blocks down to the main intersection and left over the bridge.

The Kid considers Ma's spiel a bit insulting as Grandpas been making this run since the year Ought One, but he keeps his trap shut in case Ma gets second thoughts and reverses her decision to let him go with the only living grandfather he has which is a line he memorized in case he needed to make a point Ma couldn't refute.

Sis is still staring up to the heavens that The Kid considers strange behavior since Sis is usually a straight on looker.

The Kid waves so long, and sitting up straight so Ma will be proud of him, thanks the Good Lord Grandpa selected him, not his brothers who come to think of it he hasn't seen since breakfast.

What the locals know is that Grandpa can't see ten feet in front of him, but since he is a wonderful provider for the church they daren't say anything about his driving. To play it safe they either beat an early path to church or stay indoors when Grandpa revs 'er up.

The Kid's first glimmering of trouble occurs when Grandpa backs into the street, bumping over the curb and smashing the mail box on the neighbor's lawn. Without a backward glance, the old man yells, "Tally Ho," and off they sputter and jerk as fast as the Model T can go.

Suddenly aware that his mortal remains might just not ever see the East End again, The Kid's face goes white and he plants his feet against the floor board as Grandpa zigzags between elms and oaks paying scant attention to the street while roaring down the sidewalk.

When they arrive at the main intersection the stop light is red, but it might as well have been in the next county because Grandpa not only can't locate the light, he barely remembers where the intersection is. At the last moment he jerks at the wheel and the Model T whips left headed for the bridge that is about umpteen feet above a river crashing down over a falls that is quite a sight if you're standing on the ground safe and sound. By this time The Kid is whimpering, wants to scream but his lungs are cinched up as tight as the leather on a snare drum.

Then he pulls in some air and yells, "Grandpa, we're on the SIDEWALK."

The old man smiles, jerks the T onto the road and bores ahead. Straight at the bridge they roar, Grandpa a chooging on the horn like a preacher on God's mission bringing in the sheaves.

Wooden slats resound as the T bumps across the span. The Kid casts his eyes on the rapids below, muttering Hail Mary's, envisioning Grandpa taking a sharp right through the narrow fence that protects them from the rapids below.

The old man glances at his grandson smiling a knowing smile, and across the span they roar.

On the church steps Ma stands stoically, bible in her hands, praying softly, listening apprehensively to words of anger and consternation from the congregation waiting to see if the old gent'll bring 'er in in one piece.

"Crazy old fool shouldn't be allowed on the streets. Told Herman last week the council should take the car away from him. And to think the Mrs. allowed her son ride with him. Pray for the boy, he might not have much time left."

When Grandpa chugs into the parking lot The Kid notices that except for a few cars peaking behind a stand of elms, it was empty. Which strikes him as mighty strange. The church steps are filled with people staring at them, and he wonders how they all got there without transportation. There were cars in town because he spotted a bunch of Chevys and Fords on the street when they arrived. Maybe, he decides, it's only sinners who owned cars, because everybody knows sinners shun the house of God.

Grandpa gets out spryly from the Model T and walks over to Ma, says with a twinkle in his eye, "That boy of yours is a bit skittish isn't he?"

Ma notices her youngest is kinda pale, sorta like a flapping catfish hanging from a hook that is unusual because he generally has a dare me look about him. She don't cotton to anybody casting any wimpy remarks about her brood, but coming from Grandpa, she clamps her jaw shut lest the old man decides to change his will at the last moment.

"Not taking him back home with me," Grandpa declares and marches up the steps.

Ma grabs The Kid, muttering, "I know blamed well you are not driving him home."

The rest of the week The Kid and his only living grandfather spend their waking hours together. Of an evening they'd sit on the front porch swing eating caramels that Grandpa produces magically from a paper bag that had no bottom. Between slurping down the candies the old gent goes on about the old sod and how he came over from Kilkenny as a lad just The Kid's age in 1857 arriving all by himself because his mother Anastasia died and was buried at sea. He traveled the Erie Canal alone from New York City to Rochester then walked a long way south to the farms where his sisters Julia and Kate worked as maids to a rich New York family. He boarded with Julia and was sent to school.

The Kid says, "And you were only my age?"

"Yes," says Grandpa with far away eyes.

Grandpa talks proudly about The Kid's father, and how sorry he was that his only son passed on before The Kid got a chance to know him. We named him William Judson, William for my uncle still back in Kilkenny and Judson for my best friend. I worked his father's farm on Henrietta Road, made eight dollars a month, plus room and board, and at the end of a year saved ninety-six dollars.

The old man nodded as if proud of the accomplishment.

Your father was real smart in school, and he played the violin, too. He and Belle who played the piano used to have musicals and dances in the gazebo I built next to my farmhouse. Those were wonderful times.

"Then why did Dad leave the farm?"

When his mother died the light went out him. He didn't want to work the farm any longer. And he just left. Grandpa sits silently for a while then talked about visiting his brother Richard's gravesite who died in the battle of Nashville in the Civil War.

The Kid's all ears when it comes to stories about his father, but all this business about death disquiets him, makes him wonder if that's all old men think about.

Pulling himself out of his gloom, Grandpa regales his grandson with tales of his travels all over the USA, laughing and slapping his knee and generally having a high old time remembering the swindlers who tried to sell him everything from a piece of the Grand Canyon to a lot in Death Valley. This turn about makes The Kid happy and he laughs right along with Grandpa even though he don't understand half of what the old man says. Which is probably due to the old man's false teeth slipping out just when he arrived at the punch line.

When it comes time to rev up Red's Model A for the trip back home, The Kid is kinda sad because he figured out this might be the last time he'd see Grandpa. Didn't need Ma to tell him that. Fact was he'd taken a shine to his only living grandfather.

Driving away The Kid waves back at the old man who is standing ramrod straight waving back. Even when the old man disappeared from sight, The Kid kept staring back.

For awhile he didn't have too much to say, As they plunked along Route 6 he heard, but didn't pay attention to Sis perking up the conversation with comments about this or that aunt or uncle or cousin and how well Grandpa looked. That kind of stuff.

But for some reason unknown to him he looked at Ma and Sis and Prunes and Red differently, not with his eyes mind you, but inside, and he didn't understand what he was feeling.

It wasn't until Sis poked him in the ribs and read off a Burma Shave sign that he smiled then laughed out loud that everything was okay once again.

For The Kid it was enough they were all together: Red at the wheel, Ma up front, Sis and Prunes and The Kid in back seat. Chugging along Route 6, The Kid was in a world of his own.

That Christmas eve they all sat around the tree. Ma opened the hot air register and the living room was toasty warm. The Kid listened to Sis and The Boys talking about this and that, his eyes focused on the lights and tinsel, and the tiny model of Santa's sleigh and reindeer Uncle Bill had made for him. He felt good inside.

Once Johnny had asked him what he wanted for Christmas and he said a tree would do just fine, thank you very much. Johnny couldn't believe he hadn't prepared a Christmas list, but the truth of the matter was what he really wanted was his father. He said that to Johnny, once. But he never said it to Ma or Sis or Prunes or Red. To God, but nobody else.

The tree looked the same from year to year, same old tinsel, same old lights, nothing changed, nothing added. Of course there were presents for him now what with Sis and The Boys working, but somehow, gifts weren't important.

Ma informed the brood that next year she would have the attic insulated. That brought a smile to The Kid's puss. Still owed Prunes and Red a payback for moving his sleepy body from his warm spot to one of the cold beds. Then he remembered that if it wasn't for Prunes and Red he wouldn't have received a balloon tired bike for his last birthday. Oh well, maybe he'd just forget the whole thing. What's a cold bed between brothers anyway?

He put on his winter pajamas and filled up the hot water bottle, kissed Ma and Sis good night, gave Prunes and Red a half-baked smile telling them he expected to wake up in his own bed. As he ran quickly upstairs to the Arctic attic he heard Ma asking The Boys what ever did the boy mean?

Ma had hung his stocking above his pillow. Come morning it would have an apple in the toe and an orange in the heel, and a game, and candy filling up the rest. Ma, he knew, was the best Santa in the whole world.

The attic didn't seem so cold that Christmas eve. Even though the freight trains waa, waa, waaas sounded sharper in the crystal clear air, he felt warm. And he thought good thoughts.

The trip east had been the great adventure of his life. The image of his grandfather tearing along in his old Model T was worth the price of admission. Well, one time maybe. Each year he got a Christmas dollar from his Aunt Belle, and each year he struggled writing a thank you letter to her. This year, by golly, he would think up something important to say.

Before his eyes closed he prayed that Ma and Sis and Prunes and Red and the East End would never change.

Just go on forever.

LOOKING BACK

The front cover photograph of my siblings, Sis, Bud, Jack and me, age two, and the backdrop photograph taken sometime around 1938,39 represents a timeline in our lives during the horrific years of the Great Depression.

In the early years unemployment ran as high as 25%, huge odds against Sis and my brothers getting a job, yet as the back cover photograph shows each one had a job at Deere & Co. paying each $61 a month.

Behind them in age as much as ten years I was a child during these terrible years, and even now I can't really express what they had to face. I knew not my siblings sacrifices to keep, as my mother would say, "a roof over our heads." To Helen and Jack who have gone before me and to Bud my debt to them can never be paid. And these family memories I have written are a lasting reminder of that debt.

Helen Annabelle Johnston (Sis) was not only a second mother to me, but was also the best-looking and smartest one of the Glendon tribe. I was always her little brother – she was the spoiler and I the spoilee, a relationship I enjoyed enormously. She had two children that after practicing on me, she had the spoiler business down to an art form.

She and her husband (Pete, a great guy) bought my mother's house in order that she could live her declining years in familiar surroundings tells a lot about Sis's character and devotion. The Good Lord puts special people on this earth of ours. Sis was one of those people.

She died in June 11, 1993.

William Donald (Bud, Buddy, Prunes) is studious and a great reader, traits I share with him to this day. With constant disappointments in his resume during the depression he finally got a job in a foundry, the dirtiest, hottest, sweatiest job he ever had. Getting his first week's pay he saw that his envelope contained only eleven dollars. Thinking he was due more, he asked the paymaster if there had been a mistake. No said the paymaster, that's it. He didn't argue.

Eventually at age 21 he got a pattern makers apprenticeship that opened up the future he so ardently sought. It paid $11 a week of which one dollar went for lessons and $5 to our mother. He had an entire $5 to splurge any way he desired. $5 A WEEK!

Long retired from management positions at Deere & Co. Bud represents what an active life means to maintaining good health sans pills. He spends every day at the trade he loves, and importantly, haunts various libraries for a new supply of books.

John Alfred (Jack, Jacky, Red) was the most personable of the Glendon crew. Although no one would accuse him being a bookworm, he had the most retentive mind of anyone I've ever known. He retired from a high management position at Deere & Co.- this without a high school education.

These qualities, a wonderful personality and keen mind were the basis for many of the stories in this book. He had that rare ability to create laughter when one had to ignore reality to see anything amusing in the dismal times that confronted us daily.

He joined the Marine Corps in WWII, and spent three plus years in the Pacific. Under the chapter caption *"A MATTER OF HONOR"* the photograph shows Jack with his pals Cully

Johnson and Soup Tisdale. Cully Johnson lost his life in a B-17 bombing raid over Germany, and Robert "Soup" Tisdale, a Marine, was killed in the battle of Guadalcanal. Cully and Soup are grim personal reminders of a world at war following a backbreaking depression.

Jack died on November 3, 1999

Will and Dais and Kiddos

I resented, unfairly, that Sis and Bud and Jack knew our Dad. Everything about him arrived to me secondhand – like Jack and Bud telling me that Dad pulled the engine of his touring car each winter, tearing it down and rebuilding it in the basement, this in order that the car would be in perfect running order come summer vacation and visits back east with Grandpa and our Irish relatives – or Helen talking of those same trips, especially the one just after I was born and Mom took me on the train and the three kidos went with Dad on the long drive east - just three kids and a harried father.

Or the time when the family was on one of their usual Sunday drives and Mom bet Dad a dollar that they had passed the Iowa hometown of President Herbert Hoover only to be proved wrong. Dad claimed they had yet to come to his birthplace, West Branch, Iowa. When West Branch came into view he asked her for his dollar. She refused to cough up the precious dollar. Dad, who Helen described as a soft touch, on this occasion, stood his ground and firmly insisted. Mom reluctantly, and not too happily forked over the dollar to the delight of the kidos and a family story was born. This is the personal stuff that is the essence of my Dad of which I had no share.

With the death of her, "Beloved Will," my mother faced these desperate depression years with the task of raising four children alone and without any income. Helen told me that after Dad died a local banker came to the house and gave her a bleak picture of her finances, with no prospect of improvement. "What am I supposed to feed these children with," she asked, "bricks out of the house?" Such was the reality of the Great Depression.

Shortly after our closest neighbors, knowing her uncertain future, offered to raise us children. With fierce determination she gathered us around her apron strings, said thanks but no thanks. One time a neighbor told me she was a survivor, as in life was nothing but a struggle. I doubt she thought of herself that way. The true meaning of her life - assuring the futures of Helen, Bud, Jack, and me - was the glorious fulfillment of her own life.

She was our doctor and nurse, gave us tender loving care and if that didn't work, a slug of castor oil and orange juice or maybe a mustard plaster should the occasion demand. The lingering taste of the slimy castor oil ruined orange juice for me forever. Later she switched to Father Johns. Not quite caster oil but close enough. And a mustard plaster slapped on the chest was supposed to make you well? I think not.

As a wee tyke I'd watch her from the kitchen window, all bundled up in the winter's cold pinning the washing on the clothesline. Her fingers were raw and cracked from the effort, but I always got a wave and a smile. Her smile almost made me forget the mustard plaster, but NOT the castor oil.

Jack often said, "She was the smartest woman I ever knew." I once asked her how she had made it through the depression. "Tough," is what she replied. I do not know now, nor did I know then the reality of what her, "tough," meant. She had true grit, enormous loyalty, and the gift of love that came with a hug as she dispensed one of her Scottish scones straight from the oven.

She had an uncanny knack for remembering the dates of every wedding, birth and death of all the Clan Munro from Tain, Scotland and Chicago. She wrote it all down in a date book, a present from Aunt Kate in Tain, Scotland. It is dated 1910. The cover has disintegrated and it's held together with a rubber band. But her hand is still there, keeping track of the family as always.

Without her date book, this reminiscence would have not been possible.

With the advent World War II huge changes came to our mother. Helen, Bud and Jack were married, Jack joined the Marine Corps, and when I left for the Merchant Marine Cadet Corps and the South Pacific she was left home alone, no longer the center of our lives. But with Kathy, then Sandy coming along she had a new "brood" of grandchildren to share her bountiful care and love. On top of her bedroom dresser their photos joined ours, one by one, always room for the newest one.

Lying in bed before turning off the light, she would glance at the photographs of the new generation just to make certain they were still there, or maybe wondering who the next one would be to join her galaxy. They were constant reminders of the ongoing pageant of her life. Occasionally she spoke lovingly about the Scots Highlands and the wee house where she was born, but always she faced the future with optimism.

And I spoke wrongly. She was always the center of our lives.

Her memory is a gift I cherish.

During WWII Robert R. Glendon served as a Cadet-Midshipman in the Merchant Marines on board the SS Cape Faro in the South Pacific, Atlantic, and Mediterranean theaters of operations. He subsequently was stationed in Osaka, Japan, in the 3059th Ordnance Service Company as a member of the U.S. Army of Occupation.

As a Special Agent of the FBI he ran intelligence operations targeting communist countries, and coordinated political terrorist matters including the Weather Underground. After retiring he provided negotiation advice to corporations and families in kidnapping and extortion incidents, both overseas and in country.

He has authored three novels, Faith of our Fathers, a kidnapping-spy thriller, Case Day One, an extortion-kidnapping thriller, and a murder mystery, Let The Dead Stay Buried.